The Small Hours

A Play

Francis Durbridge

A SAMUEL FRENCH ACTING EDITION

FOUNDED 1830

SAMUELFRENCH-LONDON.CO.UK
SAMUELFRENCH.COM

FOR AMATEUR PRODUCTION ENQUIRIES

UNITED KINGDOM AND WORLD
EXCLUDING NORTH AMERICA
plays@SamuelFrench-London.co.uk
020 7255 4302/01

Each title is subject to availability from Samuel French,

depending upon country of performance.

THE SMALL HOURS

First produced at the Thorndike Theatre, Leatherhead, by Bill Kenwright, on the 22nd January, 1991, with the following list of characters:

Ronnie Sheldon	Neil West
Carl Houston	Patrick Mower
George Westwood	Douglas Fielding
Vanessa Houston	Pamela Salem
Millie Decker	Sallyann Webster
Bernard Decker	Richard Walker
Ruth Wyatt	Carole Mowlem
Oliver Radford	Norman Eshley

Directed by Sebastian Graham-Jones
Design and costumes by Karen Bartlett

CHARACTERS

Ronnie Sheldon
Carl Houston
George Westwood
Vanessa Houston
Ruth Wyatt
Bernard Decker
Millie Decker
Oliver Radford

With the exception of two seats in an aircraft the entire action of the play takes place in the living-room of Carl and Vanessa Houston's apartment at *The Orchard Hotel*, near Chichester

ACT I
SCENE 1   Coming Home ... Night
SCENE 2   Several days later. 7 p.m.
SCENE 3   The following morning
SCENE 4   9 p.m. that night
SCENE 5   The next morning
SCENE 6   In the small hours of the next day

ACT II
SCENE 1   Several hours later the same morning
SCENE 2   Evening of the same day
SCENE 3   An hour later
SCENE 4   Later the same evening

Time—the present

ACT I

Coming home ... Night

The stage is in complete darkness until a subdued light reveals two seats in an aircraft. It is night and these are the only seats visible

Ronnie Sheldon dozes in the gangway seat. He is a young advertising executive, casually dressed for the long journey home. Sitting next to him is Carl Houston. Carl is an attractive man in the middle forties. It is obvious that he is bored by the journey and the book he is attempting to read

There is a long pause

Ronnie opens his eyes, fidgets, then sits upright and looks at his watch. Carl closes his book; glances at Ronnie. Ronnie takes another look at his watch, finally shaking his wrist

Ronnie What time do you make it?
Carl (*peering at his own watch*) I make it just gone nine.
Ronnie My watch must be on the blink. (*Shaking his wrist again*) Which isn't surprising, I'm on the blink myself if you ask me. (*Brief pause*) What time do we get to Singapore?
Carl Heaven only knows! It'll be in the small hours, that's for sure. (*Pause*) I didn't realize this plane stopped at Melbourne.
Ronnie No; neither did I.

Pause

Carl We were late leaving Sydney.
Ronnie Yes. Fortunately.
Carl Fortunately?
Ronnie I only just made it.
Carl (*amused*) Oh! (*He returns to his book*)

Pause

Ronnie Was this your first visit to Australia, Mr—er?
Carl Houston. Carl Houston. (*Closing the book*) Yes, it was. My sister and her husband live in Sydney and my mother joined them about a year ago. (*Pause*) Are you on holiday?
Ronnie No, I've been working in Sydney for the past six months. I'm with New World Advertising. Or rather, I was!
Carl Didn't I read somewhere that New World had pulled out of Australia?

Ronnie Yes, you did, I'm afraid.

Carl What happened?

Ronnie It's a good question! We thought we could teach the Aussies a thing or two, but it didn't work out that way. They knew every trick in the book. So, one bright, sunny morning, the entire staff got the chop. (*Indicating himself*) Including poor old Ronnie Sheldon.

Carl Oh, dear! Bad luck.

Ronnie Which is why I'm flying home now, instead of this time next year. Still—I'm not too depressed. In fact, to be honest, I shan't be sorry to get back to dirty old London. Job or no job!

Carl smiles. Pause

Do you live in London, Mr Houston?

Carl No. My wife and I have a small hotel outside of Chichester.

Ronnie (*surprised*) That's interesting. A small hotel?

Carl Yes. Well—not all that small. Thirty rooms.

Ronnie Near Chichester?

Carl Just outside. (*Looking at him*) You seem surprised, Mr Sheldon?

Ronnie I am rather. I felt sure you were something in the city. Banking. Stock Exchange. Shipping, perhaps. That sort of thing.

Carl Curiously enough, I did work in the city for a time. I was with the Maple Insurance Company. But I didn't think it showed! Not any longer.

Ronnie What made you go into the hotel business?

Carl I'd always been interested in hotels so one fine morning, aided and abetted by a cousin of mine, I borrowed a small fortune and bought *The Orchard*. Except that it wasn't called *The Orchard Hotel* in those days. It was called *The Swinging Gate*.

Ronnie *The Swinging Gate*?

Carl Yes. And don't ask me why! There wasn't a gate in sight, swinging or otherwise. Still, I should talk! There's no longer an orchard. We've turned it into a car park.

Ronnie Is your cousin in the hotel business?

Carl No, but it's about the only business he's not in. I expect you've heard of him. Oliver Radford.

Ronnie (*surprised*) Oliver Radford? Yes, of course I've heard of him! (*Amused*) "Rise above it Radford".

Carl That's right.

Ronnie He's your cousin?

Carl Yes.

Ronnie Tell me: I've often wondered. How did he come to be called that?

Carl He was interviewed on television and never stopped saying "whatever the problem, dear boy, we must rise above it". Ever since then the papers have taken the mickey out of him.

Ronnie Well, he should worry. From all accounts he's loaded.

Carl makes no comment

I expect you read his book?

Carl *Why Aren't You A Millionaire?* Yes, I read it.

Ronnie I read it twice. I got the message, but not the know-how. Still, to be fair, it was full of good advice.

Carl Maybe you should read it again.

Ronnie (*laughing*) Maybe. (*After an appreciable pause*) Did you see much of Australia whilst you were there?

Carl No. Hardly anything. I was in Sydney practically the whole time. (*A pause. Amused*) It's funny, you know. Before I went to Australia the one thing I wanted to see, more than anything else, was a Koala bear.

Ronnie (*taken-aback; staring at him*) A Koala bear?

Carl (*surprised by his reaction*) Yes. (*A moment. With a little laugh*) And I still haven't seen one.

Pause. Carl is vaguely conscious of the fact that Ronnie is still staring at him

I've heard people say they don't like Sydney. But I found it a very attractive city.

Ronnie (*hardly aware of his comment*) So did I.

Carl Wonderful situation.

Ronnie (*quietly; his thoughts still elsewhere*) Yes, wonderful ... (*He finally takes his eyes off Carl*)

Carl opens his book again, searching for the page where he left off reading. Pause. There is an atmospheric noise on the flight tannoy system followed by the voice of the Captain

Captain's voice Attention, please! Captain Goddard speaking. This is an important announcement so listen carefully ...

Carl and Ronnie look at each other

(*Nervously; clearing his throat*) Two of our passengers are armed and are extremely dangerous. One of them is with me now, on the flight deck. For the time being you must not—repeat, *must not*—leave your seats. I will try to talk to you again later.

The flight tannoy is switched off. A tense silence

Ronnie My God! We've been hijacked!

The figure of a man can now be seen emerging out of the darkness. He carries an automatic weapon and is wearing a hood and a camouflaged-style track suit

The Lights quickly fade to Black-out

SCENE 2

The living-room of Carl and Vanessa's apartment at "The Orchard Hotel". Several days later. 7 p.m.

A large, modern room on the ground floor of the building (part of a recent extension to the hotel). Comfortable chairs and sofa, tables with lamps, a hi-fi unit, drinks cabinet, etc. A desk, complete with hotel intercom system, telephones, and business accessories, stands near a full-length window which opens on to a patio and a private garden. The main entrance to the apartment is through a hallway down R, which also leads to the kitchen. Doors lead to bedrooms, dining-room, and the rest of the accommodation

George Westwood is alone in the room, quietly taking stock of his surroundings. He is in his late forties and wears a business suit

There is an appreciable pause, then Vanessa Houston enters from the bedroom

Vanessa My husband will be with you shortly.
Westwood Thank you, Mrs Houston.
Vanessa You say you're from Scotland Yard, Mr Westwood?
Westwood That's right. (*He produces a CID identity/photo-card and hands it to Vanessa*) I'm in charge of a new department. Well—fairly new. Most people, certainly the general public, know very little about us. (*Smiling*) It's a situation we tend to encourage, I'm afraid.

Vanessa studies the photograph, comparing it with Westwood

Westwood (*a moment*) If there's any doubt in your mind, Mrs Houston, please—don't hesitate to phone Scotland Yard and ask for my office. (*He indicates the phone*)

Vanessa shakes her head and returns the identity card to him

Vanessa I take it this is something to do with the hijacking?
Westwood Yes. I intended to interview your husband at the airport but got stuck in a two-mile traffic jam.
Vanessa I know how you felt. It took us ages to get home. We've only been back an hour.
Westwood How is your husband?
Vanessa He's tired, he's having trouble with his shoulder, and he's very much on edge, I'm afraid ...
Westwood Which isn't exactly surprising.
Vanessa Still, let's face it, he's lucky to be alive!
Westwood He most certainly is.
Vanessa How many casualties were there? Do you know? One paper I read said twenty, but last night on television——
Westwood A young man was shot and fourteen people lost their lives when the fire broke out. Quite a few of the passengers are still in hospital in Singapore and are likely to remain there for some time.
Vanessa What happened to the two men? The hijackers? Is it true they were killed?
Westwood Yes, both of them. (*Tiny pause*) Mrs Houston, tell me: what was your husband doing in Australia? Was it a business trip?
Vanessa No. He has a married sister in Sydney and about a year ago his mother took it into her head to join her. She was living with us at the time and we'd had, er—one or two problems.

Westwood gives a sympathetic nod

Unfortunately she hasn't settled. That's why Carl had to go out there.

Carl enters. He wears a dressing-gown over his underwear, having been lying on the bed, resting. He looks drawn and exasperated. His right shoulder is hurting him slightly

Westwood It's very good of you to see me, Mr Houston.

Carl Is it? I'm not so sure it isn't damn stupid the way I'm feeling at the moment. Anyway—what can I do for you? What is it you want?

Westwood If you'll bear with me, sir, I'd like to ask you a few questions.

Carl All right. Go ahead. But I doubt very much whether I can tell you anything you don't already know.

Vanessa indicates that Westwood should occupy one of the armchairs

Westwood (*with a little nod to Vanessa, moving to the chair*) First of all, I'd like to hear in your own words, what happened after Captain Goddard made his announcement.

Carl (*shaking his head*) I must have told this story half a dozen times in the past forty-eight hours!

Westwood Yes, sir. But not to me.

Vanessa hesitates, a shade concerned about Carl, then she sits on the sofa

Carl (*after a moment*) A man came from the back of the plane. I think he must have been hiding in one of the toilets. He was wearing a hood and was carrying an automatic rifle. Almost as soon as he appeared pandemonium broke out and a girl started screaming. He told her to be quiet and when she continued screaming he hit her across the face and grabbed hold of her hair.

Vanessa, disturbed by the story, buries her head in her hands. Carl looks across at her

Westwood Go on, sir.

Carl There was a young man, sitting just behind the girl. He jumped up and tried to get hold of the gun. There was a brief struggle and ... he was shot ...

Westwood Did anyone try to help him?

Vanessa looks up

Carl (*after a moment*) No, I'm afraid not. Everything happened so quickly ...

Pause

Westwood As I understand it, there were just two hijackers?

Carl Yes, but we—the passengers—only saw one of them.

Westwood Why was that?

Carl The other man was with the captain, on the flight deck. He stayed there the whole time.

Westwood And you never saw him?

Carl Well—that isn't strictly true, I suppose. We caught a glimpse of him when the fire started and like everyone else, he was trying to get off the plane. (*Suddenly; agitated*) Look, it's pretty obvious to me you know a great deal more about this business than I do! So would you mind telling *me* something.

Westwood What is it you want to know?

Carl What precisely did the hijackers want? What were they after? No-one told the passengers anything. Not a thing! We've been kept completely in the dark!

Pause

Westwood When the plane landed in Singapore the two men made certain demands. The authorities refused to deal with them and mounted a rescue operation instead.

Carl Rescue operation! You've got to be joking! It was a bloody fiasco! Fifteen people lost their lives including the captain and most of the crew. (*A tense pause*) You still haven't answered my question.

Westwood I'm aware of that, Mr Houston, and I'd like to answer it. Believe me I would. But I'm not in a position to do so at the moment.

Carl For security reasons, no doubt?

Westwood That's one way of putting it.

Carl Well, for your information, I'm up to here in security! Right up to here!

Vanessa rises and, moving to Carl, takes hold of his arm in an attempt to pacify him

We were questioned immediately after the abortive rescue attempt, immediately after we arrived at the hospital, and believe it or not we went through the same routine three days later when we were finally allowed to leave Singapore!

Westwood (*quietly*) Yes, I know. I've seen the report. I understand only too well how you must be feeling.

A tense pause

Carl (*less aggressive*) Now, if you've any more questions, please—let's get them out of the way so I can continue my rest ...

A slight pause, during which Vanessa returns to the sofa

Westwood You said just now, when the girl started screaming, the man with the gun told her to be quiet.

Carl Yes.

Westwood He spoke English?

Carl Yes. With a very strong accent.

Westwood It didn't occur to you that the accent might be phoney?

Carl (*surprised by the question*) Phoney?

Westwood Yes.

Carl No, it didn't.

Westwood Mr Sheldon—the man whose life you saved—doesn't agree with you, sir. According to a report we've received from Singapore, he thinks the accent was false; put on for the occasion. In fact, he goes further than that. It's his opinion the man was a European. Possibly English.

Carl I can't imagine why he thought that. I most certainly didn't get that impression. And I don't think anyone else did.

Westwood nods. Vanessa is looking at Carl, obviously curious

Vanessa Is it true you saved this man's life?

Carl hesitates

Westwood Mr Sheldon was sitting next to your husband. He panicked when the fire started and in the turmoil that followed was knocked down. Your husband, very courageously, dragged him off the aircraft.

Carl His body was blocking the exit. I had no choice. (*To Vanessa*) I was scared to hell. I hardly knew what I was doing.

Westwood When did you last see Mr Sheldon, sir?

Carl I was having trouble with my shoulder and he was in the ambulance which took me to the hospital.

Westwood Was he badly hurt?

Carl No, I don't think so. He was more frightened than anything. Almost hysterical, poor devil. Just couldn't stop talking.

Westwood What did he talk about, sir? Can you remember?

Carl glares at him, astonished by the question

Carl Of course I can remember! What would you talk about for God's sake, if you'd just been hijacked and dragged feet first off a burning aircraft?

Westwood rises

Westwood (*good-natured*) Point taken.

Carl Apart from which, like most of us, he'd lost everything. Every mortal thing, except the clothes he was wearing. And they were a write-off.

Westwood Did you lose everything, sir?

Carl Yes, I did! Every damn thing! Including a very nice handbag I'd bought my wife.

Westwood (*looking at Vanessa*) Bad luck, Mrs Houston. (*To Carl*) The handbag was in your suitcase, I take it?

Carl No. If you must know, it was in my flight bag.

Westwood With the Koala bear?

Carl stares at him, puzzled

Carl With the Koala bear?

Westwood (*smiling*) Yes.

Carl (*still staring at him; frowning*) What are you talking about? What Koala bear?

Westwood Didn't your friend, Harry Scottsdale, make you a present of a soft toy, sir? Just as you were leaving?

Carl No, he didn't!

Westwood Not when he was seeing you off, at the airport?
Carl (*exasperated*) Why would he give me a toy, for God's sake? We have no children!
Vanessa There's just the two of us, Mr Westwood.
Carl And come to that, how do you know about Harry Scottsdale? Who told you about him?
Westwood (*unruffled*) Obviously, I've been misinformed.
Carl And very badly misinformed, if you ask me! No-one saw me off at the airport!
Westwood (*surprised*) No-one, sir?
Carl (*with slightly embarrassed irritation*) I've just said no-one!

Vanessa rises and makes another attempt to calm her husband

Vanessa Who's Harry Scottsdale, darling? I've never heard of him.
Carl Yes, you have! I mentioned him on the phone. He's a friend of Oliver's.
Vanessa (*realizing he is on edge*) Yes, of course. I remember now ...
Westwood (*deciding to bring the interview to a close; very friendly*) Mr Houston, I apologize for disturbing you. Under the circumstances you've been very tolerant and I appreciate it. Do get in touch with me, if you feel I can help you in any way. You can always get me at the Yard, and I'm in the book.

Carl gives Westwood a curt nod and returns to the bedroom

Westwood turns towards Vanessa who is looking a shade embarrassed by Carl's abrupt departure

Do you think I might use your phone, Mrs Houston? I promised to let my office know when I was leaving here.
Vanessa Yes, of course.

She indicates the desk then quickly follows Carl into the bedroom

Westwood looks at his watch, then moves down to the phone. Somewhat leisurely he dials a number. Pause

Westwood (*on the phone*) Scotland Yard? Extension eighteen. ... I'm just about to leave. ... (*He looks towards the bedroom*) She seems a very nice women. ... I think he's lying. ...

Black-out

SCENE 3

The same. The following morning

Ruth Wyatt, the secretary, and acting manageress of the hotel, is on the phone. Despite an air of authority she is not an unattractive woman

Ruth (*on the phone*) Forget the invoice! We're not complaining about the invoice, we're complaining about the service. Or rather lack of it! ...

That's not true. The loose covers were due back last week! ... Friday's too late. We need them before then. ... (*Sensing victory*) What time tomorrow afternoon? ... Very well, you do that. (*Gentle sarcasm*) Have a nice day ... (*She puts the phone down, faintly pleased with herself, picks up a notebook which is on the desk and studies it*)

Bernard Decker, the Head Chef, enters from the hall. He is good looking and fully capable of switching to a certain boyish charm if he feels the effort is worthwhile. He wears his uniform, minus the hat, and carries a menu

Bernard Here's the menu you wanted to see.

Ruth continues looking at the notebook, showing her authority by deliberately keeping him waiting. Finally, she looks up and takes the menu from him

Ruth Thank you, Bernard.
Bernard Any sign of Carl?
Ruth Not yet.
Bernard What's happening, Ruth? I've barely caught sight of him since he got back. Have you talked to him?
Ruth Only briefly. But I had a long talk with Vanessa soon after they arrived. She said he was very up-tight and his shoulder was troubling him. Apparently he did something to it on the plane.
Bernard Ye gods, it's not surprising he's up-tight! Can you imagine what it must have been like on that plane?

Vanessa enters from the bedroom

Vanessa (*surprised to see Bernard*) Why, hallo, Bernard!
Bernard Good-morning, Vanessa. How's Carl this morning?
Vanessa He hasn't had a very good night, I'm afraid. He's having trouble with his shoulder. I've asked the doctor to take a look at it.
Ruth He'll feel better in a day or two, I'm sure.
Vanessa Let's hope you're right. Have you spoken to the dry cleaners, Ruth?
Ruth Yes, I've just been talking to them. They've promised to let us have the covers back tomorrow. Incidentally, Vanessa, the girls are having trouble with the computer till.
Vanessa Again?
Ruth You seem to be the only one who understands it. Yesterday afternoon one of the guests was charged six pounds eighty for a cup of coffee. Oh—and before I forget. The bank telephoned. They'd like a word with Carl. Sometime today, if possible.
Vanessa It's that new manager. Mr—whatever his name is. He just never stops asking questions.

Carl comes in from the bedroom. He appears slightly more relaxed than in the interview with Westwood, but one gets the impression that he is controlling his true feelings

Carl Who never stops asking questions?
Vanessa The bank manager. He wants to talk to you.

Carl Well, don't look so worried, Vanessa. After what I've been through I daresay I can cope with the Nat West.

Bernard laughs and Carl turns towards him

Hallo, Bernard! How are you? Sorry we haven't had a chat. We'll get round to it later.

Bernard That's all right. It's nice to have you back, Carl. How are you feeling, apart from the shoulder?

Carl I appear to have a hangover. Which is a little unfair, since I haven't had a drink for forty-eight hours.

Bernard It's those plastic avocados you eat on the plane.

Carl More than likely. I saw the article about you, Bernard, in one of the Sundays. Read it on the plane going out

Bernard I was rather pleased with it. The young lady who interviewed me was a bit of a dragon, but I managed to tame her in the end.

Carl Did you really say "Food is an important part of a balanced diet"?

Bernard Yes, I did. It wasn't original, I'm afraid, but it won her over. Millie thought it was hilarious.

Carl How is Millie?

Bernard Oh—harrassed as usual.

Carl And the boys?

Bernard They're fine.

Carl Vanessa tells me they've delivered the new freezer. Are you pleased with it?

Bernard Up to a point. It's rather on the noisy side.

Carl Oh. Well, that's no good. (*Dismissing him*) We'll take a look at it later.

Bernard goes

Ruth (*moving down to Carl with her notebook*) There's several things we must discuss, but now isn't the time, I'm sure.

Carl I gather we're not doing too well at the moment?

Ruth The hotel certainly isn't, we're only half full. But the restaurant's doing fantastic business. I'll show you the figures later. We've been turning people away almost every night this month.

Carl Why is that, do you think?

Ruth It's Bernard. He's had so much publicity recently. Apart from the article you mentioned, he's been on television twice in the past fortnight.

Carl Doing what, exactly?

Ruth Talking about himself, of course.

Vanessa He's the recognized authority on the subject. Isn't he, Ruth?

Ruth (*laughing*) That's right.

Ruth exits

Carl moves to Vanessa, gently taking hold of her

Carl I'm sorry about last night.

Vanessa Last night?.

Carl The nightmare. I must have frightened the life out of you.

Vanessa I was half expecting something of the kind.

Carl One minute I was playing tennis with Harry Scottsdale and the very next minute I was on the plane struggling with one of the hijackers.

Vanessa Who is this Harry Scottsdale? That man Westwood mentioned him.

Carl He's an art dealer in Sydney. Oliver gave me a letter of introduction to him and, believe me, he couldn't have been more helpful. Just couldn't do enough for me. He's coming over here next year. It'll be his first trip to England so I've invited him to stay with us.

There is a buzz on the intercom phone and Vanessa crosses to the desk and answers it

Vanessa (*on the phone*) Hallo? . . . Oh! Ask her to come along. (*Replacing the phone*) It's Millie.

Carl (*surprised*) Millie?

Vanessa (*returning to Carl*) Yes. She telephoned Thursday night and said she wanted to talk to us. I completely forgot she was dropping in this morning.

Carl What does she want to talk about, do you know?

Vanessa She didn't say, but I have a horrible feeling it's Bernard.

Carl What makes you think it's Bernard?

Vanessa I don't know. It was just the way she sounded.

Carl (*ominously*) Well—let's hope you're wrong.

Vanessa I've been dreading this moment. But I knew it would happen sooner or later.

Carl I can't imagine why it hasn't happened before now. How the devil he's managed to keep her in the dark this long I'll never know. Bernard really is a bloody fool when it comes to women! (*A moment*) Who is it this time? Have you any idea?

Vanessa I think it's that good-looking blonde girl who works for Oliver.

Carl Margaret—what was her name? MacKenzie? She stayed with us over Christmas.

Vanessa That's right. They've been friendly before. This is a repeat performance.

There is a slightly awkward pause

Carl I like Millie. She's a very nice little woman. But if you're right about this then we must be careful—very careful. At this moment in time we can't afford to do anything which might upset Bernard.

Vanessa I realize that. But Millie's been very good to us remember. She's helped us out on more than one occasion.

Carl All I'm saying is, it's not going to do us any good—or Millie either—if we start taking sides.

Vanessa I have no wish to take sides. But if Millie's upset then the least we can do is listen to what she's got to say.

Doorbell

Vanessa goes out into the hall. We hear the opening and closing of the front door and the sound of voices

Millie (*off*) I hope I'm not too early, Vanessa.
Vanessa (*off*) No, we've been expecting you. Come along in, Millie.

Vanessa returns with Millie Decker. She is a neatly-dressed little woman. It is obvious, from the way she clutches her handbag, that she is not looking forward to the interview

Carl (*friendly*) Hallo, Millie! How are you, my dear? (*He crosses and kisses her*)
Millie (*nervously*) Nice to see you, Carl. Did you have a nice trip?

Carl looks at her for a second or two, then bursts into laughter

Oh! Oh, I am sorry. What a silly thing to say! I do apologize . . .
Carl (*still amused*) There's no need to apologize.
Vanessa You've made him laugh, Millie. And that's quite an achievement this morning, I assure you. (*Leading her down to the sofa*) Now sit down. Can I get you anything?
Millie No. No, nothing thank you. I won't stay long. I'm sure you've a hundred and one things to see to. (*She hesitates*)
Carl Do sit down, Millie.

Vanessa sits on the sofa and pats the vacant place next to her. Millie finally sits on the edge of the sofa. Carl moves to one of the armchairs

Millie It's very kind of you both to see me. I appreciate it.
Carl You're always welcome. You know that. But you look worried. What's troubling you?

An uncomfortable silence

Vanessa What is it, Millie?

Pause

Carl Is it something to do with Bernard?
Millie (*nervously fingering the strap on her handbag*) Yes, I'm afraid it is.
Vanessa (*after a sympathetic pause*) Is he friendly with someone? Is that it?
Millie Friendly? Good heavens! Of course he's friendly with someone! You know Bernard! But that's not why I came . . .

Millie stops, having noticed the look of surprise on Vanessa's face

I know all about my husband, Vanessa.
Vanessa Oh. We—didn't realize that.
Millie I've known for some time. I just try not to think about it. (*A pause*) When I first found out about him—when a dear friend went out of her way to enlighten me—I couldn't believe it. Then one day I had it out with him. He told me it was impossible for him to change, but he had no intention of leaving me. He said he would never leave me, no matter what happened. So—in the end, I came to terms with the situation. (*Small*

pause) It wasn't easy. There were many sleepless nights. But I made the right decision. I'm sure I did. At least—that's what I keep telling myself.

Pause

Carl You still haven't told us why you're here? Why you wanted to see us?

Millie No, I haven't, have I? I came because ... you've both been very good to me. Last year when the boys were ill you went out of your way to help me. That's why I thought it only fair that you should know ... (*She hesitates*)

Vanessa Know what, Millie?

Millie Bernard's leaving you. He's giving you notice at the end of the month.

Carl (*rising*) Are you sure?

Vanessa This can't be true! Why only last week he told me how much he enjoyed working here.

Carl quickly silences Vanessa with a gesture. He moves down to the sofa, standing over Millie

Carl How do you know this? Did Bernard tell you he was going to leave us?

Millie (*a note of alarm in her voice*) No. Bernard didn't tell me. He hardly tells me anything these days, unless it's to do with the boys. I came across a copy of a letter he'd written to his accountant. It said ... (*She hesitates*)

Carl Go on, Millie.

Millie It said he'd made up his mind to leave *The Orchard* and he'd soon be giving you notice.

Carl Are you sure it said that?

Millie I'm absolutely sure. I read the letter more than once.

Carl Does Bernard know you've seen the letter?

Millie No! My goodness, no! And please—whatever happens, he must never find out!

Carl Of course not, Millie. But what's Bernard going to do, do you know?

Millie I don't know. I really don't know what's in his mind. I wish I did. (*An uncertain pause*) I'm sorry about this. I really am. I knew you'd be worried. Both of you. I was worried myself, so much so, I very nearly didn't come here ...

Carl You did the right thing, and we're very grateful. Have you mentioned this to anyone else?

Millie No. No-one ...

Carl Does Bernard know you're here?

Millie Yes. I told him I was coming. I said Vanessa had a dress she wanted me to alter.

Vanessa It so happens I have. (*Getting up*) I'll drop it in on you this evening.

There is a brief, awkward pause, then Millie rises

Carl How did you get here, by bus?

Millie No, a friend of mine gave me a lift. She's waiting for me.

Carl (*making towards the hall with them*) You've done us a favour. And it was very thoughtful of you.

Vanessa And don't worry. No-one will know about this. Will they, Carl?
Carl Of course not! This is just between the three of us. And if you hear anything else, please don't hesitate ... Come and talk to us. ...

Millie gives a somewhat frightened little nod

And take care of yourself, my dear.

Vanessa and Millie exit together

Carl's expression immediately changes; he is looking distinctly worried

Vanessa returns

Vanessa What do you make of that?
Carl We're in trouble! Deep trouble! For the life of me I don't see how we can stay in business without Bernard. If it wasn't for the restaurant we'd be in the red. And Bernard *is* the restaurant.
Vanessa Is it money, do you think?
Carl I can't honestly see how it could be. He had a very substantial bonus, at the beginning of the year. (*Pause*) I wonder if he's been offered a job in London? It's possible, after all the publicity he's been getting recently.
Vanessa (*shaking her head*) Bernard doesn't like London. He's told me so on more than one occasion. (*A worried hesitation*) What's the best thing to do, Carl? Should we tackle him, do you think? Without mentioning Millie, of course.
Carl No, I don't think so. That might be a mistake at this stage.

Ruth enters. She is carrying an account book

Carl Yes, Ruth?
Ruth I'm sorry to disturb you, but a Mr Sheldon's arrived and insists on seeing you.

Carl stares at her for a moment, obviously surprised

Carl A Mr Sheldon?
Ruth Yes.
Vanessa (*to Carl*) Surely, that's the man that was on the plane with you?
Carl (*to Ruth*) He's in the hotel?
Ruth Yes. He's staying the night. He's in Room Sixteen.
Vanessa Did you know he was coming?
Carl (*shaking his head*) No. (*To Ruth*) When did he book the room?
Ruth He didn't. He just arrived.
Carl (*after a moment's hesitation*) Ask him to come along ...

Doorbell

Ruth I rather fancy he's already here. He seems a very persistent young man. (*She turns towards the hall*)
Vanessa (*stopping her*) I'll go, Ruth.

Vanessa goes out

Ruth turns back and offers Carl the account book

Ruth I've brought you last month's figures.

Carl doesn't hear her: his eyes are on the hall

Carl (*suddenly; seeing the book*) I'm sorry. What was that, Ruth?
Ruth I thought you might like to see last month's accounts.
Carl Yes, of course. Put them on the desk.

Ruth crosses and puts the book down

There is the sound of the front door and Vanessa and Ronnie can be heard in the hall

Vanessa (*off*) Mr Sheldon?
Ronnie (*off*) Yes.
Vanessa (*off*) I'm Vanessa Houston. Carl's wife . . .
Ronnie (*off*) Oh—I'm delighted to meet you, Mrs Houston.
Vanessa (*off*) Do come in.
Ronnie (*off*) Thank you.

Vanessa enters with Ronnie Sheldon

Ronnie's clothes are now more formal and he is certainly well groomed. But he appears a little less sure of himself: he looks like a man who hasn't completely recovered from his recent ordeal. Carl crosses down to him, holding out his hand

Carl This is a pleasant surprise, Ronnie.
Ronnie (*a shade nervous; shaking hands*) I'm going to the theatre in Chichester this evening and, since I very much wanted to see you again, I decided to stay the night.
Carl I'm glad you did. Oh—I think you've met Miss Wyatt?
Ronnie Yes, indeed. Miss Wyatt . . .
Ruth I hope you enjoy your stay here, Mr Sheldon.
Ronnie Thank you.

Ruth smiles at him and goes

Carl When did you get back?
Ronnie Late last night.
Carl I looked out for you. I thought we might have been on the same plane.
Ronnie I should have been, but at the last minute the hospital insisted I have another check-up.
Vanessa Were you badly hurt?
Ronnie I wasn't hurt at all, Mrs Houston. I was just in a state of shock. (*To Carl*) I'm afraid I made rather an exhibition of myself both in the ambulance and at the hospital.
Carl Nonsense, of course you didn't! You were no different from anyone else. We were all badly shaken.
Ronnie That's an understatement, if ever I heard one! (*A moment*) It wasn't until the next day, when I was talking to one of the passengers, that I suddenly realized I owed my life to you. (*To Vanessa*) What do you say to a man who, at great risk to himself, drags you off a burning aircraft?

(*With a nervous smile*) "Thank you very much, old chap. I'll do the same for you next time" . . .

Carl Your body was blocking the gangway. I had to get you out of the way. That's all there was to it.

Ronnie (*shaking his head*) You saved my life, and I want you to know I'm very conscious of the fact. And, needless to say, very grateful.

Vanessa Is that why you came here, to thank my husband?

Ronnie (*after a tiny hesitation*) It was the main reason. Yes.

A faintly awkward pause

Vanessa Let me get you some coffee, Mr Sheldon.

Ronnie Er—thank you, no, Mrs Houston.

Carl (*indicating an armchair*) Well—sit down, Ronnie.

Vanessa sits on the sofa and Ronnie moves to one of the chairs

Were you questioned before you left Singapore?

Ronnie Questioned? The authorities have never stopped questioning me! And not only in Singapore. We'd no sooner landed at Heathrow than a man called Westwood cornered me. I was with him almost an hour.

Carl He interviewed me.

Ronnie (*surprised*) Did he? I didn't realize that. (*After an uneasy pause*) I don't know who this man Westwood is, but whoever he is, one thing's for sure! He's certainly interested in you.

Vanessa In Carl?

Ronnie Yes. In fact, to be perfectly frank, Mrs Houston, I had the impression he was more interested in your husband than the hijackers.

Carl What makes you say that?

Ronnie Well, first of all, he wanted to know what we'd talked about on the plane. Whether you'd mentioned a particular friend of yours. Someone called Harry . . . I think he said Scottswell . . .

Carl Scottsdale. Harry Scottsdale.

Ronnie Yes, that's right. Harry Scottsdale. I said I'd never heard of him. He then asked me what I thought was a very odd question. He wanted to know if we were sitting next to each other during take-off.

Carl (*after a moment's consideration*) Come to think of it, we weren't.

Ronnie That's right. But why ask that question? (*To Vanessa*) When I got on the plane I found myself wedged between a giant of a man and a girl wearing the most awful perfume. Fortunately, several people disembarked at Melbourne so I had a word with the Steward. He took pity on me and moved me to where Carl was sitting on his own.

Carl I remember. I was dozing and you were full of apologies.

Vanessa's eyes are on Ronnie, obviously curious

Vanessa What else did Mr Westwood ask you?

Ronnie He wanted to know what happened to Carl's flight bag.

Carl But he knows what happened to it! I told him!

Vanessa (*to Carl*) It was left on the plane?

Carl (*a shade exasperated*) Of course it was left on the plane, Vanessa! Ronnie's body was blocking the gangway, the aircraft was on fire, and all hell was let loose! Do you think I had time to worry about my flight bag?

Vanessa (*rising*) I'm sorry, darling . . .

Ronnie By this time I was getting very tired of Mr Westwood, so I told him—in no uncertain terms—that I wasn't prepared to answer any more questions.

Carl I know exactly how you felt!

There is a buzz on the intercom phone and Vanessa answers it

Vanessa (*on the phone*) Yes? . . . I see. . . . Thank you, Ruth. (*Putting the phone down, to Ronnie*) I'm sorry, Mr Sheldon, but will you excuse us? Carl's having trouble with his shoulder and the doctor's arrived.

Ronnie gets up

Ronnie (*to Carl*) It's not serious, I hope?

Carl No, no. I'm pretty sure I've pulled a muscle. Look—why don't you have a drink with us this evening before going to the theatre?

Ronnie That's very kind of you.

Carl Let's all meet in the bar, about six.

Ronnie is looking at Carl, hesitating, as if about to say something

Vanessa Is there something else, Mr Sheldon? Something else you wanted to tell Carl?

Ronnie No, it was just that—I shall look forward to this evening.

Ronnie goes

A slight pause

Vanessa Why was he hesitating, Carl?

Carl (*a suggestion of apprehension in his voice*) I don't know. I don't know, Vanessa. Your guess is as good as mine. (*Starting to take off his jacket*) Tell the doctor I'm in the bedroom.

Carl continues to remove his jacket as he exits

Vanessa stares after him, surprised and not a little puzzled by his manner

The Lights fade to Black-out

SCENE 4

The same. 9 p.m. that night

Carl is at his desk looking at various letters, accounts, etc. Ruth is standing by his side holding a mass of correspondence which has already been dealt with

Carl (*staring at a letter*) Who on earth are the Track-record Tractor Company?

Ruth They make tractors ...

Carl You could have fooled me ...

Ruth Their head office is at Basingstoke. According to Bernard they're a very wealthy outfit.

Carl Oh! Well, in that case, go ahead and write them. Tell them we don't usually cater for conferences but we'll be pleased to consider their request. (*He hands her the letter*) Ask for complete details. Number of people requiring accommodation, etc.

Ruth nods

And you'd better alert Bernard. They'll probably want to see a menu.

Ruth Very well. (*Picking up the rest of the letters from the desk*) How's your shoulder? Is it any better?

Carl Yes, it's fine now. I've been doing some exercises and whatever the trouble, it seems to have righted itself. I wish now Vanessa hadn't sent for the doctor, although to be fair he did suggest the exercises.

Ruth Vanessa's out, I take it?

Carl Yes, she's with Millie. She should be back shortly. (*Rising, but not moving from the desk*) When you write to the Basingstoke people don't forget to tell them if they want any printing done we must have at least five days' notice.

Ruth I've made a note of it.

Ruth exits

Carl sits again and turns his attention to various papers on the desk. He has taken a folder out of one of the drawers and is about to study its contents when Ronnie's voice is heard in the hall

Ronnie (*off*) It's important, Miss Wyatt! Very important, I assure you!

Ruth enters with Ronnie Sheldon

Ruth Mr Sheldon would like to see you, Carl.

Carl (*surprised*) Why, hallo! (*Rising and leaving the desk*) I thought you were at the theatre?

Ronnie I—I changed my mind.

Carl Why was that?

Ronnie looks at Ruth

Thank you, Ruth.

Ruth goes

Pause

Ronnie (*slowly, turning towards Carl*) I'm sorry?

Carl I asked you why you'd changed your mind about going to the theatre?

Ronnie I suddenly realized I'd seen the play before.

Carl (*not believing him*) Oh, I see.

Ronnie (*a shade unsteady; his hands trembling*) Twice. T-twice before. (*Small pause*) *A Man For All Se-Seasons* ...

It suddenly dawns on Carl that Ronnie has been drinking

Are we alone?

Carl makes a show of looking around the room

Carl It would appear so.

Ronnie I mean—are we likely to be disturbed?

Carl It's possible. My wife's out at the moment, but I'm expecting her back at any minute. (*Curious*) What's on your mind, Ronnie? Why do you wish to see me?

Ronnie (*emotionally*) You saved my life.

Carl immediately protests

(*Stopping him*) You did! You know you did! So I had to see you. I had no choice! (*A tense pause*) There's something you ought to know. Something I must tell you. I should perhaps have told you this before now, in Singapore perhaps, but—I've been so frightened.

Carl Frightened?

Ronnie Yes. That's why I've been drinking. I thought if I had a few drinks, just a few ...

Carl What is it? What is it you want to tell me?

Ronnie is still hesitating

Is it something to do with the hijacking?

Ronnie Yes.

Carl Then why didn't you tell me about it this morning? Or this evening, whilst we were in the bar?

Ronnie Your wife was with you on both occasions and I didn't want her to hear what I've got to say.

Carl Why not?

Pause. They take each other in

Ronnie Do you remember, on the plane, when we were chatting, just making conversation, you said ... The one thing you wanted to see in Australia, more than anything else, was a Koala bear?

Carl (*puzzled*) Yes, I remember.

Ronnie is staring at Carl, a deeply-troubled look on his face

Ronnie Why did you say that?

Carl (*bewildered*) Why?

Ronnie Yes. Why did you make that comment? Why mention a Koala bear?

Carl I don't know. It just came into my head.

Ronnie You had no other reason?

Carl No. What other reason could I have had? (*Mystified; a shade irritated*) Look—what is this? What's on your mind? Tell me!

Pause

Ronnie You're in danger, Carl. Great danger!

Carl I am?

Ronnie Yes. In a matter of days—maybe sooner—someone will try to kill you.

Carl (*stunned*) Kill me? Why should anyone want to kill *me*?

No response

And who is this person anyway?

Ronnie I—I can't tell you that! I daren't!

Carl (*quietly; after a watchful pause*) I'm sorry. I don't believe you. I don't believe a word of this.

Ronnie You've got to believe me!

Carl You've had too much to drink, my friend. Besides which, it's obvious you're still suffering from the after effects of the hijacking.

Ronnie No! No, it's not that! I swear it's not that! (*Heatedly*) You've got to take this warning seriously! You've got to!

Carl I'll take it seriously if you'll tell me who this person is and why they want to kill me.

A strained silence

Ronnie (*finally*) They want to kill you because of what you said to me.

Carl What I said to you?

Ronnie Yes.

Carl When?

Ronnie On the plane.

Carl (*incredulously*) About my wanting to see a Koala bear?

Ronnie (*wrought up*) Yes!

A brief moment, then Carl bursts into laughter. Then suddenly, seeing the worried expression on Ronnie's face, his laughter stops. Pause

Carl You should see someone, Ronnie. If you have a good doctor, consult him. Straightaway.

Ronnie You think it's that simple?

An uncomfortable pause

(*Fatalistically*) Well—I've warned you. I've said what I came to say! If you refuse to believe me there's nothing else I can do. Nothing! (*He turns towards the hall and is about to leave*)

Vanessa rushes into the room. She looks tired, wet, and exasperated

Carl (*alarmed*) Vanessa! What's happened? (*Moving down to her*) Have you had an accident?

Vanessa No, not exactly, but coming back from ... (*Surprised to see Ronnie*) Oh—hallo, Mr Sheldon!

Ronnie Mrs Houston ...

Vanessa (*to Carl*) No, I haven't had an accident. But what a journey! What a dreadful journey!

Carl takes hold of her

Carl (*concerned*) Are you all right?
Vanessa Yes. I've had a nasty shock, that's all.
Carl Why? What happened?
Vanessa I was driving back from Millie's and was half way down Quarry Lane when a stone shattered the windscreen. For a moment, I couldn't see a thing. On top of which it was pouring with rain and I was getting drenched. Fortunately, I was able to pull into the side of the road. I was quite shaken, Carl.
Carl I'll bet you were!
Vanessa Finally, I smashed a hole in the windscreen and drove home.
Carl You should have phoned me. I'd have picked you up.
Vanessa The nearest phone box was miles away on the main road.
Ronnie (*after a small pause*) Are you sure it was a stone that hit the windscreen, Mrs Houston?
Vanessa (*surprised by the question*) Why, yes! Although it's strange you should ask that. At one point I thought I heard what sounded like a shot. But that's absurd, of course. It must have been a stone ...

A brief silence

Carl Which car were you in, Vanessa?
Vanessa Yours, I'm afraid. It was already starting to rain when I left and the BMW was on the drive. I'm sorry, darling. I should have taken the Escort.

A pause, during which the two men avoid looking at each other. Finally, Carl kisses Vanessa on the cheek and moves towards the drinks cabinet

Carl You're not hurt, that's the main thing. Now let me get you a drink. I'm sure you could do with one.
Vanessa No, thank you. All I want at the moment is to get out of these clothes and into a nice hot bath. Good-night, Mr Sheldon.
Ronnie Good-night, Mrs Houston.

Vanessa hurries into the bedroom

There is a tense pause, then Carl slowly turns and looks at Ronnie

Ronnie Now do you believe me?
Carl (*quietly*) Yes, I believe you.
Ronnie (*with almost a suggestion of relief in his voice*) Good. Now perhaps you'll take my warning seriously. (*He moves towards the hall*) You'll want to talk to your wife, so come to my room tomorrow morning and we'll continue this conversation then.

Ronnie exits

The Lights quickly fade to Black-out

Scene 5

The same. The next morning

Ruth is tidying the desk, re-arranging various papers, filing receipts, etc.

Carl comes in from the bedroom. He looks tense; worried. On seeing Ruth he makes a determined effort to be pleasant

Carl What time do you make it, Ruth?

Ruth (*glancing at her watch*) It's just gone ten. When are you picking Vanessa up?

Carl She said she'd be finished by half-past, but you know hairdressers. We're due at the hospital at eleven. (*Crossing to the hall*) I'm just going along to have a word with Mr Sheldon. If the bank telephones tell them I'll be in touch with them later in the day.

Ruth (*stopping him*) But Mr Sheldon's left.

Carl (*turning; surprised*) Left?

Ruth Yes. He paid the bill and checked out just after eight o'clock.

Carl Are you sure?

Ruth I'm quite sure.

Slight pause

Carl Did he leave a message?

Ruth I don't think so. In fact, I'm sure he didn't. He appeared to be in a hurry. Just couldn't get away quick enough.

Pause

Carl Have we got his address?

Ruth I'll check with reception.

Carl Yes, please do that, Ruth.

Ruth exits

Carl stands for a moment deep in thought and not a little puzzled. Finally, he turns towards the desk, picks up the phone, and dials. There is a pause, whilst the number is ringing out

Oliver Radford enters. He is an affluent-looking man in the early fifties. He wears a smart coat and carries an impressive-looking case. His manner is nearly always charming, but he is fully aware of his own importance

Carl (*surprised; putting the phone down*) Why, Oliver! I was just ringing your office! (*Moving down to him*) How are you, Oliver? I'm delighted to see you!

Oliver How am I? My dear chap, what's more to the point, *how are you?* Miss Wyatt tells me you're just off to the hospital.

Carl I did something to my shoulder on the plane, but it's better now. Much better. Unfortunately the doctor's arranged an X-ray and I can't very well get out of it.

Oliver My God, did you have a lucky escape? And it was quite a cliff-hanger in this neck of the woods, I might tell you. It took Vanessa the best part of twenty-four hours to find out what had happened to you.

Carl I'm sure.

Oliver Is it true you lost all your things when the plane caught fire?

Carl Yes. Everything. Including that marvellous flight bag you gave me.

Oliver Not to worry, we'll get you another one.

Carl It's good to see you, Oliver. You'll stay to lunch, of course?

Oliver Thank you. But that's not possible, I'm afraid. I have a meeting in Portsmouth at two-thirty. (*Putting his case down*) I gather you saw quite a bit of Harry Scottsdale whilst you were in Sydney?

Carl Yes, we became great friends. And my sister and her husband adored him. (*With barely concealed anxiety*) Oliver, I'm pushed for time, but do stay. We shouldn't be all that long at the hospital and I very much want to talk to you.

Oliver stares at him, a shade puzzled

Oliver What's happened? Are you in some sort of trouble?

Carl (*after a brief hesitation*) I'm worried. Desperately worried—and I'd very much like your advice.

Oliver (*eyeing him*) Boy, you really are worried! What's the problem?

Carl hesitates, then glances at his watch

Carl When the plane caught fire one of the passengers, a young man called Ronnie Sheldon, suddenly panicked and in the turmoil that followed was knocked to the ground. Fortunately I was able to grab hold of him and drag him to safety.

Oliver You saved his life?

Carl Well, in a way, yes ...

Oliver What d'you mean, in a way? You obviously did!

Carl Sheldon came to see me yesterday, to thank me for what happened, and whilst he was here he said he had something to tell me. Something of importance ...

Oliver (*curious*) Go on.

Carl He said my life was in danger—great danger—and it was only fair that he should warn me of the fact.

Oliver What did he mean, your life was in danger?

Carl He said that within a matter of days, possibly sooner, someone would try to kill me.

Oliver (*taken aback*) Kill you?

Carl Yes.

Oliver Did he tell you who the person was?

Carl No.

Oliver Did he tell you why they wanted to kill you?

Carl Yes. But his explanation didn't make sense. Not to me at any rate.

Oliver (*with almost a note of belligerence*) Well, who is this Ronnie Sheldon anyway? And what does he do, apart from scaring the hell out of people?

Carl He was with New World Advertising. But the poor devil's been made redundant.

Oliver Advertising! Good grief, you mustn't take any notice of those people! You can't believe a word they say! They live in a dream world. If I were you, Carl, I'd forget it. I'd put the whole thing out of my mind.

Carl Just "rise above it", in fact?

Oliver (*with a little laugh*) You said it, dear boy, not me!

Carl (*with an unmistakable note of anxiety*) Oliver, I do wish you could stay. I've so much to tell you. Last night, for instance . . . Someone fired a shot at my car. Vanessa was driving. She'd been to see a friend of hers and was on the way back when suddenly——

Oliver (*stunned*) You're not serious! You can't be!

Carl It's true, Oliver.

Oliver Was Vanessa hurt?

Carl No—and fortunately she didn't realize what had happened.

Oliver Did you report the incident to the police?

Carl No.

Oliver Why ever not?

Carl Vanessa didn't know about the warning I'd received from Ronnie Sheldon and—I didn't wish to frighten her. The poor darling's had a bad time recently. Apart from being worried about the hijacking she's had to cope with the fact that I've been concerned, very concerned, about my mother. On top of which—as you well know—she didn't want me to go out to Australia in the first place. (*After an anxious glance at his watch*) Oliver, I do wish we could talk about this later . . .

Oliver stares at him, struck by the note of desperation which had entered his voice. Pause

Oliver (*making a decision*) All right! Get off to the hospital. I'll wait for you.

Carl (*relieved*) Are you sure?

Oliver Yes, I'm sure. You've made me curious. Damn curious! I want to know what this is all about! And don't rush, take your time. I'll be here. (*He indicates the desk*) But this is going to cost you! I shall be on your phone the best part of the morning.

Carl Go ahead, please! Make as many calls as you like.

Carl goes

Oliver takes off his coat, carefully folds it and places it on a chair. Having done this, he picks up his case and, crossing to the phone, dials. Pause. The number is engaged and after a little while, and with a gesture of irritation, he rings off and moves to the sofa. He sits, operates the combination lock on his case and takes out a bulky-looking document. He frowns over this

Oliver (*muttering to himself*) Lawyers . . . ! Blasted lawyers!

Bernard enters bearing a tray with coffee, etc.

Bernard I heard you were here, Mr Radford, so I've brought you some coffee.

Oliver Oh! That's very welcome. Thank you, Bernard.

Bernard puts the tray down on one of the tables

Oliver has returned to his document

Bernard (*at the tray*) Do you take cream, sir?
Oliver No. Black, please. No sugar ...

Bernard pours the coffee and takes it down to him

(*Taking the cup, hardly raising his eyes from the document*) Thank you.
Bernard (*after a tiny hesitation*) Do you mind if I join you, sir?

Oliver looks at him, a little surprised

Oliver No. No, of course not.
Bernard I usually have a cup of coffee at this time of the morning.
Oliver By all means ...

Bernard returns to the tray and leisurely pours himself a cup of coffee, adding sugar and cream. As he crosses to one of the armchairs Oliver puts the document down. Pause

I thought of you last week-end.
Bernard Oh? In what connection?
Oliver I was in Geneva and had lunch at the *Richemond*. Didn't you once tell me you worked there?
Bernard Yes, I did. It was the first job I had on the Continent. Fancy your remembering.

Oliver smiles. They drink their coffee. There is a long pause, during which Oliver stares at him

Oliver What's your problem, Bernard? What is it you want to talk about?
Bernard What makes you think I have a problem?
Oliver I can spot one a mile away. What is it, my friend?
Bernard (*after a moment's consideration*) May I tell you something, in the strictest confidence?
Oliver Oh, dear! I've never been impressed by confidentiality. In my experience confidences frequently turn into gossip. If I receive a letter marked "Strictly Private" I invariably let my secretary open it. However—there's always the exception. What is it you wish to tell me in confidence?
Bernard I'm leaving here. I shall be giving Carl notice, probably this weekend.
Oliver Really? (*Eyeing him*) That's interesting. May I ask why you're leaving?
Bernard I intend to start a business of my own.
Oliver A business of your own?
Bernard Yes. I propose opening a restaurant.
Oliver Here, in Chichester?
Bernard No, no! I wouldn't dream of doing that ...

Oliver I'm delighted to hear it.

Bernard That would be most unethical.

Oliver It would indeed. So where do you propose to open this restaurant?

Bernard I've seen a place at Bath. It's a small hotel at the moment, just bed and breakfast, but it could very easily be converted into a restaurant.

Oliver At a cost, I imagine?

Bernard Yes, at a cost.

Oliver Are you serious about this? Or is it just a whim, a flight of fancy you indulge in from time to time?

Bernard I'm very serious. I couldn't be more serious. I realize of course that Carl won't be too happy about this. On the other hand if I don't make a move now ...

Oliver Let's leave Carl out of this for the moment. You're an excellent chef, Bernard. Quite outstanding ...

Bernard Thank you.

Oliver But what makes you think you can run a business of your own?

Bernard (*quite pleasant*) What makes you think I can't?

Oliver Have you had any managerial experience?

Bernard No.

Oliver Can you read a balance sheet?

Bernard No.

Oliver Then I would most certainly have second thoughts if I were you. (*A moment*) How much are they asking for this place at Bath?

Bernard Two hundred and ninety thousand.

Oliver Have you got two hundred and ninety thousand pounds?

Bernard No, I haven't.

Oliver Won't you find it a little difficult to raise that sort of money? It's frustrating I know, but banks insist on collateral these days. I take it you know what collateral is?

Bernard Yes, I know. But I don't propose to go to the bank.

Oliver You don't?

Bernard No.

Oliver Then who's going to lend you the money?

Bernard No-one.

Oliver No-one? (*Puzzled*) I'm afraid I don't understand. If you haven't got the money, and you don't propose to borrow it, how can you buy the property?

Bernard The answer's quite simple. Much simpler than reading a balance sheet, I'm sure.

Bernard finishes his coffee then, watched by Oliver, he rises and takes his cup to the tray

(*Turning; almost matter-of-fact*) You're going to give me the two hundred and ninety thousand pounds, Mr Radford. You're going to make me a present of it.

Oliver rises dumbfounded

Oliver I—am—going—to—give—you—two hundred and ninety thousand
... (*Bursting into laughter*) You're crazy! You're out of your tiny mind,
dear boy! (*Finally controlling his amusement*) Give me *one* good reason,
just one, why I should give you a hundred pounds, let alone two hundred
and ninety thousand?

Bernard moves slowly down to him

Bernard I'll do better than that. I'll give you three good reasons

*Oliver looks at him, suddenly struck by the seriousness of Bernard's expression
and his tone of voice*

Oliver Three reasons?

Pause

Well—go ahead ...

Bernard One: I know the reason—the real reason—why you gave Carl a
letter of introduction to your friend Harry Scottsdale ...

Oliver Go on ...

Bernard Two: I know why Ronnie Sheldon was on that particular flight
from Sydney.

Oliver is now staring at him with barely-concealed hostility

Oliver Do you? Go on, my friend ...

Bernard Do I have to give you the third reason? (*Pause*) I know about the
Koala bear.

Black-out

SCENE 6

The same. The small hours of the following morning

*The curtains are drawn and the room is in partial darkness, the only light
coming from a table lamp*

*Carl—tense in manner, deeply troubled—is seen pacing the room. He is
wearing a dressing-gown over pyjamas. There is a half-smoked cigarette in his
hand*

*After a little while he stops pacing, crosses to the drinks cabinet, disposes of his
cigarette, and is about to open a bottle of Scotch when Vanessa enters from the
bedroom*

Vanessa I wondered what had happened to you! (*Pause*) I thought you were
in the bathroom.

Carl replaces the bottle and moves down to her

Carl I couldn't sleep.

Vanessa You should have taken something. (*Small pause*) Is your shoulder still troubling you?

Carl No. Go back to bed, Vanessa.

Vanessa What is it, Carl? What's worrying you?

Carl Nothing! Now, please! Leave me alone and go back to bed.

Vanessa (*concerned*) What is it? Tell me! I want to know. (*She moves nearer him*)

Carl I've told you! Nothing's worrying me. I just can't sleep, that's all.

Vanessa Something's the matter, and I've a right to know what it is.

Carl I feel restless and terribly on edge the whole time. But it'll pass. Now please, do as I say.

Pause

Vanessa Is the Bernard situation worrying you?

Carl No! If Bernard leaves, he leaves! We'll survive somehow!

Vanessa Then what is it? (*Taking hold of his arm*) I'm not going back to bed until you tell me what this is all about. You've been desperately worried all day. And I want to know the reason!

A pause. Vanessa still holds his arm, earnestly staring at him

You know me, Carl. I won't let up! You'll have to confide in me sooner or later. You might just as well do it now!

A brief silence, then Carl gently releases himself

Well?

Carl Last night when you were driving back from Millie's someone tried to kill me.

Vanessa reacts immediately

(*Stopping her*) Please, Vanessa! It was my car you were driving. It was raining heavily and difficult to see. They thought I was at the wheel.

Vanessa (*with total disbelief*) What are you saying? That someone fired at the car?

Carl Yes.

Vanessa That it was a bullet that shattered the windscreen?

Carl nods

I can't believe that's what happened!

Carl You said yourself you thought you'd heard a shot ...

Vanessa Yes, but—I just don't believe this, Carl!

Carl It's true, Vanessa. Ronnie Sheldon warned me something of the kind would happen. That's why he came here last night.

Vanessa (*staggered*) Ronnie Sheldon warned you?

Carl Yes.

Vanessa But why on earth should anyone want to kill *you*?

Carl is hesitating, undecided whether to confide in her or not

Carl (*finally*) He said my life was in danger because of something I'd said to him on the plane.

Vanessa Did he tell you what it was?

Carl We were talking about Australia and I said—by way of conversation—that I'd always wanted to see a Koala bear but somehow I'd never got around to seeing one.

Vanessa (*puzzled*) Well?

Carl That's it.

Vanessa (*staring at him*) And that's why someone wants to kill you? (*Incredulously*) But that's ridiculous! He was joking, Carl! He must have been.

Carl (*shaking his head*) He wasn't joking. He was serious. He couldn't have been more serious. (*Taking hold of her arm*) Well—now you know why I've been worried and difficult to deal with during the past twenty-four hours. I'm sorry if I've taken it out on you. (*Gently; releasing her*) I intended to talk to Oliver about this, but unfortunately . . .

Vanessa (*surprised*) Oliver? Why Oliver?

Carl He's always helpful. He looks at a problem from every possible angle.

Vanessa But Oliver's just a business man. An entrepreneur.

Carl That's as maybe, but his advice is always worth seeking. I was bitterly disappointed when we got back from the hospital and found his note saying he'd had to return to London.

Vanessa Yes, well—if I were in your shoes I wouldn't waste five minutes talking to Oliver.

Carl No? Then what would you do? (*Quickly, before she can answer him*) You don't have to tell me! (*Exasperated at the thought*) Believe me, Vanessa—the very last thing I feel like doing at the moment is having a heart to heart talk with *your* Mr Westwood.

Vanessa You may not feel like it, but you've got no choice.

Carl is about to retort, but something in her voice makes him hesitate

Westwood questioned Ronnie Sheldon, remember—and not long afterwards Sheldon turned up here. Now what would you think, if you were Westwood? You'd very quickly jump to the conclusion that the pair of you were in cahoots over something.

Carl That's as maybe! Nevertheless, I don't want anything to do with Westwood. Not if I can possibly avoid it.

Vanessa (*shaking her head*) But you can't avoid it. Not any longer! You've got to talk to someone in authority about what happened last night, about what Ronnie Sheldon told you. And surely, *my* Mr Westwood as you call him, is the obvious choice.

An awkward silence

Why are you hesitating?

Carl I just don't want to get involved with Westwood! Now, please—let's leave it at that, Vanessa!

Vanessa (*persistent*) Why don't you want to get involved with him?

Carl Because he doesn't believe a word I say, that's why!

Vanessa That's not true.

Carl I'll go even further. I have a horrible feeling he thinks I had something
to do with the hijacking.

Vanessa That's nonsense, Carl.

Carl Then why question Ronnie Sheldon about me? And why on earth all
those questions about Harry Scottsdale?

Vanessa Carl, I know what you've been through. I know you've had a
terrifying experience—but please, don't get things out of proportion. It's
Westwood's job to ask questions. You've got absolutely nothing to worry
about so far as he's concerned, I'm sure.

Carl is wrapt in thought for a moment

Carl You could be right. We'll talk about it at breakfast.

Vanessa Yes, let's do that. Now get your drink, then come to bed.

Carl nods and crosses to the cabinet

Carl Would you like one?

Vanessa No, but I think perhaps I'll make some tea.   .

Carl I should, if you feel like it.

Vanessa goes into the kitchen

*Carl opens a bottle of Scotch, thoughtfully mixes himself a drink, and
carries the drink into the bedroom*

Long pause

*A Man can be seen emerging from behind the curtains. He wears dark
trousers and a black anorak. A mask covers his features*

*After a glance towards the kitchen the Man moves slowly across the room in
the direction of the bedroom, then stops. There is a tense moment before he
produces a switchblade knife from the pocket of his jacket and flicks open the
blade. The Man slowly approaches the bedroom*

Vanessa enters and gives a terrified scream, dropping the tray she's carrying

*The Man springs angrily in Vanessa's direction, determined to silence her.
Vanessa immediately reacts, making a wild dash for the hall*

Carl comes racing out of the bedroom

As the Man turns, Vanessa stops in her tracks, freezing

A tense pause. The two men are now facing each other

Carl Who are you? What is it you want?

The Man draws dangerously near Carl, the knife raised, ready to strike

(*To Vanessa*) Phone the police!

Vanessa hesitates

(*With quiet authority, his eyes on the knife*) Do as I say!

Vanessa makes a nervous move towards the desk and the Man instinctively half turns and looks at her. This is what Carl had hoped for and he takes instant advantage of the moment, springing forward and striking the knife out of the Man's hand

Whilst the two men are locked in a struggle for the knife, Vanessa reaches the phone and is dialling for help

Carl has gained possession of the knife and the struggle is continuing when the Man gives a sudden and totally unexpected cry; it is the cry of a man in intense pain, the full weight of his body falling against the knife Carl is holding. Carl releases his hold on his attacker, staring in horror at the blood pouring down the Man's anorak

Hearing the cry and seeing the Man fall to the ground, Vanessa drops the phone and rushes towards Carl

Vanessa What happened?

Carl (*bewildered*) I don't know! He suddenly cried out! One minute he was struggling and then ... Get a towel, Vanessa! Quickly!

Vanessa disappears into the bedroom

Carl kneels down and begins a careful examination of the Man. A long, tense pause. He completes his examination and rises

Vanessa returns with a towel and a first-aid box

(*Looking across at her*) He's dead ...
Vanessa No! Oh, no! He can't be!
Carl (*softly*) He's dead, Vanessa.
Vanessa He must have had a heart attack! (*Moving towards him*) You didn't kill him! You can't have done!

A strained silence

Who is he, Carl?

Carl, almost in shock, shakes his head—then, after a nervous hesitation, he removes the mask. There is a tiny pause, as he stares at the Man in utter astonishment

You recognize him?
Carl Yes. It's Harry Scottsdale!

CURTAIN

ACT II

Scene 1

The same. Several hours later that morning

The telephone is ringing

Ruth rushes into the room from the hall, puts several letters down on the desk, and picks up the phone

Ruth (*on the phone*) Hallo? . . . Yes? . . . Who is that? . . . (*Annoyed*) Look—this is the third time you've telephoned! There's nothing more I can tell you! . . . Mr Houston's not available. . . . I don't know! I don't know when he'll be able to talk to you—if at all! (*She slams the receiver down*)

Bernard enters. He is wearing a suit, having just come on duty

Bernard (*bewildered*) Ruth, what on earth is going on? There are reporters all over the place! What's happened?

Ruth A crazy man broke into the apartment and attacked Carl with a knife . . .

Bernard Good God!

Ruth There was a struggle and, as I understand it, the man was killed.

Bernard When was this?

Ruth About three o'clock this morning. I suddenly heard voices so I came down to the apartment. Carl was with Vanessa and they were talking to a police inspector. The dapper little man, who has a drink in the bar occasionally.

Bernard Tom Bradshaw. But tell me: how was Carl?

Ruth He was badly shaken, as you can well imagine. The inspector allowed him to make a phone call to someone in London. Then both he and Vanessa went down to the police station. They were there for hours. It must have been after seven when they got back here.

Bernard Where are they now? Resting?

Ruth Vanessa is. She started one of her migraines, poor darling. Carl had a quick breakfast and drove into Chichester for a meeting with his lawyer.

Bernard What a terrible thing to have happened! Anyway, if Carl needs me, or there's anything I can do, you know where I'll be.

Bernard goes

Pause. Ruth is tidying up the desk

Bernard returns

There's a Mr Westwood here. He says he has an appointment with Carl.

Ruth Carl hasn't any appointment that I know of. It's a ploy. Get rid of him, Bernard, he's from one of the newspapers.
Bernard I don't think he is. He says Carl telephoned him.

Ruth looks at Bernard, hesitating

Ruth Westwood, did you say?
Bernard Yes. He's driven down from London.
Ruth (*after a brief pause*) Ask him to come in.

Bernard goes

Ruth, a shade puzzled, consults the files, but her thoughts are elsewhere. She is looking towards the hall

Bernard enters with Westwood

Westwood Miss Wyatt?
Ruth Yes.
Westwood My name is Westwood. Mr Houston telephoned me early this morning and said he wished to see me.
Ruth I'm afraid Mr Houston isn't here. He had to go into Chichester.
Westwood And Mrs Houston?
Ruth She's resting at the moment, she hasn't been feeling well. Shall I tell her you're here?
Westwood No, please! Don't disturb her. (*He looks at his watch*) When are you expecting Mr Houston?
Ruth That's difficult to say. There was an unfortunate ... incident ... here last night and his movements are a little uncertain.
Westwood Yes, I know about the incident.

Bernard moves to leave but Westwood notices the movement and stops him

Don't go, Mr Decker!

Bernard turns, somewhat surprised

Westwood (*pleasantly*) We've met before.
Bernard Really, sir? I don't recall——
Westwood My wife and I had dinner here, a few weeks ago.
Bernard Oh ...
Westwood I complimented you on your moussée de brochet.
Bernard (*he doesn't remember*) Yes, of course!
Westwood (*to Ruth*) It was the best mousse I've tasted. Out of this world. My wife even went so far as to say it was as good as hers.
Bernard (*laughing*) Praise indeed!
Westwood (*after a moment*) I take it you were both here when this incident occurred?
Ruth I was. I live in the hotel. But Mr Decker wasn't.
Bernard I knew nothing about it until I arrived just five minutes ago.
Westwood I see.
Ruth (*hesitant*) Mr Westwood, forgive my asking, but—are you with Scotland Yard? Are you the man that interviewed Carl—Mr Houston?

Westwood Why do you ask?

Ruth Mrs Houston told me what happened and I was wondering whether you were ... *that* Mr Westwood ... ?

Westwood (*smiling*) Yes, I'm *that* Mr Westwood, Miss Wyatt.

Carl enters

Carl (*briskly, on seeing Westwood*) I'm sorry to have kept you waiting. I had an appointment in Chichester.

Westwood I've only just arrived.

Carl (*to Bernard, somewhat abruptly*) You wanted to see me?

Bernard It was just that, I wondered if I could help in any way?

Carl Not at the moment. (*Dismissing him*) Thank you, Bernard.

Bernard goes

Ruth Several newspapers have telephoned and some of the reporters have been trying to interview the staff. I think it might be a good idea, Carl, if you had a word with them.

Carl (*cutting her short*) Don't worry about the newspapers, Ruth. Did you manage to get hold of Mr Radford?

Ruth He's somewhere on the Continent at the moment, but I spoke to his secretary. She's going to get him to ring you. I impressed upon her it was urgent.

Carl gives her a dismissive shake of the head

Ruth exits

Carl (*to Westwood*) I imagine you know by now, what happened here this morning?

Westwood Yes, I know. I called in the police station. The inspector was very co-operative.

Carl (*somewhat aggressive*) I'm glad to hear it. I hope you'll take a leaf out of his book.

Westwood I'll do my best.

Carl Well—you can start by putting me in the picture!

Westwood Since you sent for me, Mr Houston, don't you think you should be the one to do that?

Carl No, I don't! If, as you say, you've spoken to the inspector ...

Westwood I did more than that. I read the statement you made and had a long talk with the chief constable.

Carl Then there's nothing I can tell you about this morning's incident that you don't already know. So now, perhaps, you'll satisfy my curiosity. (*A moment*) When I arrived at London Airport you asked me a great many questions. The significance of which escaped me. One was about a Koala bear ...

Westwood (*watching him*) Yes, I remember.

Carl Why did you ask that question?

Westwood Why?

Carl Yes. Why did you want to know if Harry Scottsdale had given me a soft toy, in the shape of a Koala bear?

Westwood (*after a moment*) Don't you know why, Mr Houston?

Carl No, I don't!

A brief, slightly awkward silence whilst they take each other in

After you'd questioned me you interviewed Ronnie Sheldon, and shortly afterwards Mr Sheldon came to see me.

Westwood nods

Much to my astonishment he told me that my life was in danger because of something I'd said to him on the plane. Something, believe it or not, about a Koala bear.

Westwood Go on, Mr Houston.

Carl I thought he was talking nonsense. That he'd had too much to drink. I very quickly discovered otherwise. Two attempts have already been made on my life and unless I'm very much mistaken there's likely to be a third. (*Angry; almost carried away*) Why? Why is someone trying to kill me? You know the answer to that question and I want to know what it is!

Pause. Westwood is staring at Carl in disbelief

Westwood (*quietly*) Are you telling me that—you don't know why your life is being threatened?

Carl That's precisely what I'm telling you!

Westwood And you expect me to believe that?

Carl Why shouldn't you believe it?

Westwood Because you're lying, my friend. You've never stopped lying! You lied to me and you lied to the inspector.

Carl The inspector?

Westwood Yes.

Carl When?

Westwood When you made your statement. You said you were astonished to find that Harry Scottsdale was in this country.

Carl But I was! I was amazed!

Westwood I don't believe that! You must have known he was over here! You saw a great deal of him whilst you were in Australia.

Carl I don't deny that. But I hadn't the slightest idea he was in this country.

Westwood Harry Scottsdale arrived in London several days ago. He flew into Heathrow on a Qantas flight from Sydney, picked up a cab at the airport, and was driven straight to a hotel in Kensington.

Carl I know nothing about that!

Westwood Don't you, Mr Houston? My guess is, he contacted you—or you contacted him—and you had a row over something.

Carl That's not true!

Westwood I think it is! And I think that's why he came here in the early hours of this morning!

Carl is shaking his head in disbelief

Carl But that's just not true! My wife saw what happened. The man was wearing a mask. I hadn't the slightest idea who he was or what he looked like.

Westwood He wasn't wearing a mask when the police arrived.

Carl Of course he wasn't, I'd removed it. But the inspector saw the mask, I gave it to him.

There is a pause. Westwood is giving him a long, intent look

Westwood Mr Houston, unless I'm mistaken, within twenty-four hours from now you'll be in trouble. Real trouble. So I'm going to stick my neck out and give you a piece of advice. For your wife's sake, as well as your own, I only hope you'll take it.

Carl (*no longer able to control his feelings*) I don't want your advice! I simply want you to answer the questions I asked you five minutes ago! Why is my life in danger? Who is it that wants to kill me?

Vanessa enters from the bedroom as Carl finishes speaking

She immediately senses the atmosphere that exists between the two men

Vanessa What is it, Carl? What's happened?

Carl (*making a desperate attempt to control his feelings*) Nothing's happened. It's all right, Vanessa. (*Moving towards her and taking hold of her*) Are you feeling better?

Vanessa Yes. I've had some sleep, thank goodness.

She looks at Westwood as Carl releases her

Westwood I'm sorry you're not feeling well.

Vanessa I've had a migraine. I get them from time to time.

A brief silence

Westwood Your husband's in a very serious situation, Mrs Houston. I'm sure you realize that?

Vanessa Yes, I realize it. We both do. That's why he sent for you.

Westwood Unfortunately there's nothing I can do to help him.

Vanessa turns towards Carl, concerned

He's reached a stage where no-one can help him, I'm afraid. No-one, that is, except himself.

Carl (*flaring up again*) And what the hell does that mean?

Westwood It means that at some point—and before it's too late—you've got to start telling the truth. (*To Vanessa; an unmistakable note of concern in his voice*) For your sake, if for no other reason, do try and convince him of that fact, Mrs Houston.

Westwood exits

There is a tense pause

Vanessa (*anxiously*) What's going to happen to you, Carl?

Carl I don't know. I just don't know!

Vanessa What did Westwood have to say? (*Pause*) Tell me!

There is an uncomfortable hesitancy on Carl's part, before answering her

Carl He told me that Harry Scottsdale arrived in London several days ago and was staying at a hotel in Kensington.
Vanessa Well? (*A brief, yet tense pause*) Well?
Carl He's convinced I knew Harry was over here.
Vanessa But you didn't know!
Carl Of course I didn't! I hadn't the slightest idea he was in London! If I'd known he was here I'd have told you. We'd have talked about it!

A pause. Vanessa is gazing at him, steadily

Well—don't you believe me?
Vanessa Yes. Yes—I believe you ...
Carl But?
Vanessa There's no "buts" ...
Carl (*keyed up*) But, Vanessa? (*An appreciable pause*) Well?
Vanessa I think—I can't help thinking—that you're keeping something back. That there's something you haven't told Westwood. Something you haven't told either of us.
Carl About what?
Vanessa I'm not sure. About Harry Scottsdale, perhaps ... and what happened in Australia.

Pause

Carl There's only one thing I haven't told you. And it's not important.
Vanessa Let me be the judge of that.

Pause. It is obvious that Carl is trying to make up his mind whether to confide in her or not

Carl (*reaching a decision*) One night, about a week before I left Sydney, I arranged to have dinner with Harry. To my surprise, when I arrived at the restaurant he had a couple of girls in tow. One of the girls—a New Zealander called Julie Tyson—fell for me in quite a big way. She just never stopped telephoning and sending messages. The morning I was leaving Harry was due to drive me to the airport but the wretched girl talked him out of it.
Vanessa What are you saying? That this girl took you to the airport?
Carl Yes. I tried to get out of going with her. I made every excuse in the book. But—no way!
Vanessa But why didn't you tell Westwood this when he first questioned you? He asked you if you'd been seen off by anyone.
Carl She didn't see me off! She simply gave me a lift to the airport.
Vanessa It's the same thing, surely?
Carl (*intense*) It's not the same thing, Vanessa!
Vanessa Nevertheless, you should have told Westwood about her. It was absolutely stupid of you.

Carl I was tired and exasperated and above all I didn't want to give *you* the wrong impression.

Vanessa The wrong impression being that you were friendly with the girl? Is that it?

Carl Yes.

Brief pause

Vanessa Were you friendly with her?

Carl What are you asking me? Whether I had an affair?

Vanessa (*in as ordinary a voice as she can manage*) Did you?

Carl No, of course I didn't! I only saw her twice. Once at the restaurant and the morning she drove me to the airport.

As he moves away from her there is a buzz on the intercom phone. The buzz is repeated and Vanessa finally takes her eyes off him and crosses to the desk

Vanessa (*on the phone; impatiently*) Yes? . . . What is it, Ruth? . . . All right, I'll take a look at it. (*She rings off*) The computer's on the blink again.

Carl (*turning back to her*) The blasted thing's always on the blink! We shall have to get rid of it.

Short silence

Vanessa (*unable to control her curiosity*) What was she like?

Carl Like? Who?

Vanessa This girl. Was she attractive?

Carl Look, Vanessa! I'm in enough trouble at the moment without your imagination getting out of hand! There's only one thing you need to know about Julie Tyson. I didn't like her! In fact, I hated her! I hated her voice, her manner, the clothes she wore, every damn thing about her! Now, please, darling, let's leave it at that!

Vanessa stares at him for a moment, hesitating, as if about to question him further. Then, changing her mind, she exits

There is an uncertain pause, then Carl crosses the room and opens the window. He is facing the open window, taking deep breaths, and exercising his shoulder when, to his surprise, he sees someone approaching the house from across the patio

Bernard comes into view. He is wearing outdoor clothes

(*Surprised*) Why, hallo, Bernard!

Bernard Can you spare a moment?

Carl (*puzzled by Bernard's attire*) Well—yes. Come along in.

Bernard enters

What is it, Bernard? Is there a problem?

Bernard Yes, I'm afraid there is. I've got to take the day off, Carl. It's a confounded nuisance but I just couldn't get out of it.

Carl Oh! (*Pleasantly*) Well, if you've got to take the day off—you've got to take the day off. Have you alerted the kitchen?

Bernard Yes. Not to worry. Everything is under control.

Carl (*after a moment*) Millie's well, I hope?

Bernard Millie? Yes, she's fine. Oh! This hasn't anything to do with Millie. I've had a phone call from a friend of mine in Bath and I've got to drive over there.

Carl To Bath?

Bernard Yes. To be truthful, he's not exactly a friend. I'm involved in a property deal and he's a local builder.

Carl A property deal? You're not thinking of moving house, are you, Bernard?

Slight pause

Bernard Er—yes, as a matter of fact, I am.

Carl But surely you're not going to live in Bath? You'd spend the whole day travelling.

Bernard Oh, dear! I was hoping I wouldn't have to go into that. Not this morning.

Carl If it's something I should know, I wish you would go into it. I'd rather hear it now, than later.

Bernard (*smiling*) Would you, Carl?

Bernard decides to sit in one of the chairs. He appears very sure of himself

All right. But what I'm about to say will come as something of a shock, I'm afraid. The fact is, Carl—I shall be leaving here at the end of the month.

Carl (*none too friendly*) You're giving us notice? Is that it?

Bernard That's one way of putting it, I suppose.

Carl What other way is there? (*Pause*) What are you going to do when you leave here?

Bernard I'm going to open a restaurant of my own.

Carl In Bath?

Bernard Yes.

Carl When did you reach this momentous decision?

Bernard I've been thinking about it for some time.

Carl Don't you think you should have talked to me first? We might have worked something out.

Bernard There was very little point in talking to you. For a long time it was just a pipe dream. I didn't think I could raise the money. Then suddenly, quite out of the blue, I found that I could.

Pause

Carl Well, I'm sorry you're leaving, Bernard, and I'm even more sorry that you didn't have the good grace to tell us about this sooner.

Bernard I'm sorry, too, but it wasn't possible.

Carl Have you thought this thing through? Do you realize what you're letting yourself in for?

Bernard Yes, and I'm looking forward to it.

Carl I wonder if you'll look forward to it when you start repaying the mortgage?

Bernard The question of a mortgage doesn't arise. I've managed to raise the money.

Carl (*surprised*) You've raised it?

Bernard Yes.

Pause

Carl It's none of my business, of course, but—what sort of money are we talking about?

Bernard (*after a brief hesitation*) There's no reason why I shouldn't tell you. Two hundred and ninety thousand ...

Carl (*staggered*) Two hundred and ninety thousand? And you've raised that amount privately?

Bernard Yes. But that's just for the property. I shall need another fifty thousand. But I don't think that will be too difficult to raise. I've got some gilt-edge I can cash in and I've a couple of things I'm thinking of sending to Christies. (*Almost as if it has just occurred to him*) Also—I've got something which, curiously enough, should interest you, Carl. (*He starts feeling in his pockets*)

Carl Your news has hardly put me in a buying mood, Bernard. But what is it? What is it you're trying to sell me?

A moment, then Bernard finally finds what he is looking for

Bernard It's a cassette.

Carl (*puzzled*) A cassette?

Bernard (*rising; pleased with himself*) Yes. (*He puts the cassette he is holding on to the table*)

Carl (*after a moment*) Why would I be interested in a cassette?

Bernard You'll know when you've listened to it. (*With a glance at his watch; dismissing the subject*) Carl, I'm sorry about today, because the restaurant's fully booked. But I'll get back as quickly as I can.

Carl (*slowly; his thoughts elsewhere and his eyes on the cassette*) Yes, you do that, Bernard.

Bernard exits on to the patio

A pause, then Carl moves to the table and picks up the cassette. He stares at it for several seconds; his manner somewhat strained. Finally, he crosses to the hi-fi unit. He switches it on, inserts the cassette, and presses the play button. He stands in front of the instrument, with his back to the rest of the room, staring down at the tape

The following is heard on tape. There is a very long pause before a telephone number starts ringing out. Loud and persistent. The ringing continues for some time before the phone is answered. Then two voices are heard: a Girl's voice, and the voice of Carl Houston—or someone giving an excellent impersonation of him

Girl's voice (*brisk; business-like*) Kensington Royal——

Carl's voice Is that the *Kensington Royal Hotel*?

Girl's voice Yes, it is. Can I help you?

Carl's voice My name is Houston. I'd like to speak to Mr Scottsdale.

Girl's voice (*after a moment*) Mr——? Would you repeat the name, sir?
Carl's voice Scottsdale. Harry Scottsdale.
Girl's voice One moment. (*A fairly long pause*) Are you sure Mr Scottsdale's staying with us?
Carl's voice Yes, I'm sure.
Girl's voice When did he arrive, sir?
Carl's voice As I understand it, late last night.
Girl's voice (*after a brief pause*) Ah, yes! Here we are! He's in Room One-Two-Eight. I'll put you through.

A pause. We hear the extension number ringing out. Pause

There appears to be no reply from his room.
Carl's voice (*a worried tone*) No reply?
Girl's voice I'm sorry, sir.
Carl's voice May I leave a message?
Girl's voice Yes, certainly.
Carl's voice Tell Mr Scottsdale I received his letter, but I can't keep the appointment. It's totally out of the question.
Girl's voice I'll make sure he gets your message, Mr Houston.
Carl's voice Please do. It's very important!
Girl's voice No problem, sir. Thank you for calling.

There is the sound of the girl ringing off. The tape ends

Carl has been listening to the cassette with increasing anxiety. As the tape finishes there is an unmistakable look of despair on his face. Eventually he removes the tape, switches off the hi-fi unit, puts the cassette in his pocket and turns

  Vanessa appears from the hall where she has been standing, quietly listening to the tape

Carl freezes; staring at her in astonishment

Carl Did you hear that?
Vanessa Yes, I heard! (*Giving vent to anger*) You lied, Carl! You lied to Westwood! You lied to the inspector! And you lied to me!

The Lights fade quickly to Black-out

SCENE 2

The same. That evening

The curtains are drawn and the lights are on

Voices are heard coming from the hall

Carl enters with Millie who is carrying a dress in a plastic cover

Carl (*irritated*) I'm sorry not to be more helpful, Millie, but I just don't know when Vanessa will be back. I don't even know where she's gone. She left the apartment this morning and I haven't seen her since.
Millie Oh. (*A shade embarrassed by Carl's irritation*) Well—perhaps you'll give her this dress.

Carl Yes, of course. (*He takes the dress from her and drapes it over the back of the sofa*)

Millie I'd finished the alteration and since I wanted to see Bernard I thought I'd deliver it.

Carl I'm afraid you're unlucky on both counts. Bernard isn't here either. He's taken time off and he hasn't returned yet.

Millie Oh! I didn't realize that. (*A moment*) Well, I won't keep you, Carl.

Carl Incidentally, you were right about Bernard. He's given us notice. He's going to open a restaurant of his own somewhere in Bath.

Millie Yes, I know. He told me all about it at breakfast. (*Hesitant*) I shall be sorry to leave here, Carl, you know that. Very sorry. But it could be worse, I suppose. Bath's a very nice town.

Carl It is indeed. But please, my dear, sit down.

Millie sits on the sofa

What did Bernard tell you? What did he say, exactly?

Millie He said he'd be giving you notice but it would be some time before we'd be moving house. Which was a bit of a relief, I must say. The thought of moving terrifies me. You've no idea how much hi-fi stuff those kids have got. Noel's room looks like Dixons.

Carl Did Bernard tell you how much the restaurant was costing him?

Millie No. I asked him but all he said was, "Don't worry, everything's taken care of." (*Shaking her head*) Bernard's been rushing around like a crazy thing during these past weeks and he's hardly ever off the phone. He was talking to someone in Amsterdam at seven o'clock this morning.

A brief hesitation

I hate to say this about my husband, Carl, because in spite of everything, I'm very fond of him. But he's changed. He's quite different from how he used to be. It's all this publicity he's been getting recently. It's gone to his head. It really has, Carl. Also . . . (*She hesitates*)

Carl Also what, Millie?

Millie still hesitates

Millie (*finally*) Nothing. I really shouldn't trouble you with my worries.

Carl You're not troubling me. Anything to do with Bernard interests me, you know that. (*Slight pause*) Go ahead! Please, Millie.

Millie He's been seeing that girl again. The one that works for Mr Radford. Margaret MacKenzie. I thought it was all over between them, but I was mistaken. (*A shrug*) I don't mind him having an affair with her. Heaven knows, I'm used to that by now. But she's such a bad influence on him.

Carl In what way?

Millie She's cleverer than he is. A great deal cleverer, and yet she plays up to him like mad. Makes him feel he can't do a thing wrong. (*A sigh*) Still, one can't have everything. He's awfully good with the boys. He really is. (*Getting up*) Carl, I mustn't keep you any longer.

Carl That's all right, my dear. (*Thoughtfully*) Millie, tell me: who was Bernard talking to on the phone this morning? Do you know?

Millie No, I'm afraid I don't.

Carl Was it a man or a woman?

Millie I really don't know, Carl. (*A moment*) I—I think it was a man, but I'm not sure.

Carl gives an understanding little nod and moves nearer the hall with her

Vanessa enters

Vanessa Hallo, Millie! I heard you were here . . .

Millie I've brought your dress back.

Carl Vanessa, where the devil have you been?

Vanessa (*completely ignoring Carl*) My word, you've done the alteration quickly.

Millie It wasn't difficult once I got started.

Carl is staring at Vanessa, distinctly annoyed

Vanessa (*a friendly dismissal*) Well—thank you, Millie. You must let me know what I owe you.

Millie Don't be silly! I enjoyed doing it. The collar should be perfectly all right now.

Vanessa I'm sure it will be.

Millie Well—if it isn't, you must let me know.

Millie, now aware of the feeling that exists between Vanessa and her husband, glances at Carl, then goes

Carl (*moving down to Vanessa*) I've been telephoning all over the place! I wondered what on earth had happened to you!

Vanessa still avoids looking at him and makes for the bedroom. Carl realizes that she intends to ignore him and he swiftly moves between her and the bedroom door

Vanessa Let me pass!

Carl It's eight o'clock! It was just after eleven this morning when you left here. Where have you been all this time?

Vanessa Carl, will you please let me go into the bedroom?

Carl (*keyed up*) No! Not until we've talked!

Vanessa Can't you get it into your head that I just don't want to hear any more of your lies! Why do you think I walked out on you?

Carl, overwrought, has grabbed hold of her

Carl You've got to listen to me! We've got to talk about that phone call!

Vanessa Carl, let go of me!

Carl (*tightening his grip on her; carried away*) I won't let go of you! I won't release you, not until you promise to listen to me!

Vanessa struggles, unsuccessfully, to release herself

We've got to talk! We've just got to!

Vanessa For God's sake, have you taken leave of your senses? (*She continues struggling; intensely angry*)

Carl I just want you to hear what I've got to say! That's all I'm asking!
Please, Vanessa . . .

Vanessa gradually stops struggling. Pause

Carl (*almost a note of desperation in his voice*) Don't you realize, if you insist
on ignoring me I just won't know what to do, or who to turn to! I shall be
utterly and completely lost.

Pause

Vanessa I'm sorry. Now, please leave me alone, Carl.

*A tense moment, then Carl releases her. Vanessa turns away from him and
straightens her dress. She glances at him and hesitates as if momentarily
undecided what to do*

Then Vanessa picks up the dress on the sofa and goes into the bedroom

*Carl is despondent. He sinks into one of the armchairs and partly buries his
head in his hands. Long pause. The telephone rings. Carl slowly looks up, then
rises, and crosses to the desk*

Carl (*on the phone*) Hallo? . . . (*Suddenly, taken by surprise*) Oliver! Where
are you? . . . (*Tense pause*) That depends. . . . How much do you know?
What have you heard? . . . (*A long pause; listening intently*) That's not the
whole story, but it's more or less what happened. Who put you in the
picture? . . . Yes, I know, Mr Westwood! Is he still with you? . . . I see. . . .
(*Pause*) Oliver, tell me: did you know Harry was over here, because I
certainly didn't! . . . Yes—I was too. Staggered! I told the police that but
they didn't believe me. . . . Am I what? . . . My God, of course I am!
Wouldn't you be, if you were in my shoes? . . . (*A tense pause*) I was just
about to suggest that. We'll talk later. (*He rings off*)

*Carl moves down to a box on the table and slowly helps himself to a cigarette.
He stares at the cigarette, his thoughts still on the conversation with Oliver. He
is searching for a lighter*

Vanessa appears. She looks more composed and is now wearing a housecoat

Carl suddenly senses that she is in the room and quickly turns

Vanessa Who was that on the phone?
Carl (*putting the cigarette down*) It was Oliver. He's at Heathrow.
Vanessa Did he know about Harry Scottsdale?
Carl No. He was completely in the dark. But he isn't any longer. Westwood
was at the airport, waiting to interview him.
Vanessa Why would Westwood want to interview Oliver?
Carl It was Oliver who introduced me to Harry Scottsdale remember.
Oliver's on his way here. We've a devil of a lot to talk about so he's
staying the night. (*A slightly awkward pause*) Vanessa, I don't wish to
quarrel with you—believe me, I don't—but didn't you believe *anything* I
told you this morning?

Vanessa I believed what you said about Bernard and the cassette, but I didn't believe your story about Harry Scottsdale. How could I believe it after listening to that tape? You knew he was in London! You must have known! You tried to phone him!

Carl (*barely restraining himself*) I did not! The voice on the cassette sounds like me, it sounds remarkably like me, I admit that——

Vanessa You could hardly do otherwise!

Carl —But it's not me, Vanessa! Quite apart from the voice, the tape doesn't make sense. Never, at any time, did I receive a letter from Harry Scottsdale.

Vanessa What are you saying? That someone impersonated you?

Carl Yes, Vanessa! That's the only possible explanation!

Vanessa stares at him for a moment, obviously in two minds about this explanation, then she turns and looks thoughtfully towards the hi-fi unit

Ruth enters. She is carrying a large box which has been carefully packaged

Ruth Excuse me, Carl. This parcel has just arrived.

Carl What is it?

Ruth (*puzzled*) I don't know. I really don't know what it is.

Vanessa Who's it from?

Ruth It doesn't say. It's simply addressed to Carl and marked "Personal".

Carl It was delivered by hand?

Ruth Yes. A man on a motor bike brought it.

Ruth puts the parcel down on one of the chairs. Carl moves down to the chair, taking a closer look at it

It could be from the printers, I suppose. We've ordered copies of the new wine list.

Vanessa They wouldn't deliver at this time of day, surely?

Ruth It's unlikely.

Vanessa looks at the parcel, then at Carl. She realizes that he is suspicious

Carl What did the messenger look like?

Ruth What they always look like. Something from outer space! He had a radio blaring away and wore the usual gear.

Slight pause

Carl Did you sign for the parcel?

Ruth Yes.

Carl How?

Ruth gives Vanessa a slightly puzzled look

Ruth What do you mean, Carl?

Carl Did he offer you a book with other names in it?

Ruth No, just a slip of paper. Why?

Pause

Carl (*quietly; his eyes still on the parcel*) Thank you, Ruth.

Ruth looks at Carl, curious. She is on the point of questioning him, then changing her mind, exits

Pause

Vanessa You're thinking of what Ronnie Sheldon said? The warning he gave you?

Carl (*quietly*) Yes, I am.

A pause, then Carl picks up the parcel and cautiously examines it. Pause

Vanessa (*nervously*) Don't open it! Let the police take a look at it before you do anything.

An uncomfortable silence

Carl It's not terribly heavy. (*Pause*) This isn't from the printers. (*He holds the parcel closer to himself, as if listening for a sound of some kind*)

Vanessa (*watching his face*) What is it? Can you hear something?

Pause

Carl (*slowly*) It's probably my imagination. (*A tense pause, then he suddenly makes a decision*) You're right! I'll let the police deal with it!

Vanessa Then take it into the garden! (*She quickly crosses the room, draws back the curtains, and opens the window*)

Carl is about to carry the parcel into the garden

(*Holding his arm; restraining him*) Wait a minute!

Carl What is it?

Pause

Vanessa There's someone coming!

Pause

Westwood appears at the window

(*Taken-aback*) Why—hallo, Mr Westwood!

Westwood (*to Carl*) I was on my way to the hotel, sir—in the hope that you might spare me a few minutes.

Carl stares at him, puzzled by his friendly manner

Carl Well, in that case, you'd better come in.

Westwood enters the room

Westwood Thank you, that's most kind of you. (*Seeing the parcel*) Oh! So it's arrived then——

Carl (*astonished*) Did you send this?

Westwood My department did, but I didn't intend it to get here until I'd seen you. Unfortunately I had an interview at London Airport which took longer than expected.

Carl moves to the desk and puts the parcel down

Carl Well, since you're here, and you sent the parcel, perhaps you'll satisfy our curiosity by telling us what's in it?

Westwood I'd rather you open it. But first, there's something else I'd like to deliver.

Carl (*curious*) Oh?

Westwood (*with obvious sincerity*) An apology.

Carl An apology?

Westwood Yes, Mr Houston.

Carl looks at Westwood, wondering whether to take him seriously

Vanessa Does this mean you've changed your mind about my husband?

Westwood I'm afraid I've had to change my mind about quite a few things during the course of today. So far as your husband's concerned, let's just say my judgement has been—well, somewhat at fault.

Carl (*after a brief moment*) Very well. I'll accept your apology. (*With sudden authority*) But on one condition!

Westwood Oh? And what's that, sir?

Carl You stop prevaricating and answer the questions I asked you this morning! Who is it that's trying to kill me? And why?

A brief pause

Westwood That's fair enough, I guess, under the circumstances. But my story will take a little time. So first—I suggest you open that parcel.

Carl returns to the desk and picks up a stilleto-type letter opener. As he goes to work on the parcel Westwood stands quietly watching him, waiting to see his reaction. It takes Carl a little while to remove the wrapping paper. Finally he is able to see inside the box

Vanessa What is it, Carl?

A stunned Carl slowly takes a flight bag out of the box and holds it up for her to see

It's your flight bag!

Carl But it can't be! I left my bag on the plane! I know I did! It was destroyed. It must have been ...

Westwood (*quietly*) Look inside it.

Carl quickly zips open the bag and stares at the contents

Carl (*to Vanessa*) I was wrong! (*Incredulously*) It is my bag! These are my things!

Vanessa One of the passengers must have rescued it whilst you were helping Ronnie Sheldon.

Carl I can't believe that's what happened! There was pandemonium. No-one would have been remotely interested in rescuing my flight bag.

Westwood You're quite right. And no-one did rescue it. For the simple reason your flight bag wasn't on the plane.

Carl (*adamant*) But it was! I know it was! I had it with me the whole time.

Westwood Not your bag, Mr Houston. (*A moment*) I want you to think back to what happened the morning you left Sydney.

Carl (*after a thoughtful pause*) Harry Scottsdale was due to pick me up but at the last minute he couldn't make it, so he sent a friend of his instead. A girl I couldn't stand called Julie Tyson.

Slight pause

Westwood Go on. And what happened when you arrived at the airport?

Carl I tried to find a porter, but I was unlucky. So I went in search of a trolley.

Westwood And then?

Carl I collected my bags, thanked Miss Tyson for the lift and ... (*He stops, suddenly remembering something*)

Both Vanessa and Westwood look at him

Westwood You collected your bags?

Carl Yes.

Westwood From the boot of Miss Tyson's car?

Carl No. (*Slowly*) That's just what I was thinking. She'd taken my things out of the boot and they were ... on the pavement ... waiting for me ...

Westwood Including the flight bag?

Carl nods

Thank you, sir.

Vanessa (*to Westwood puzzled*) Does this mean Carl's flight bag was left in the car and that he picked up a duplicate one?

Westwood Yes, Mrs Houston.

Carl (*indicating the bag*) Then where the devil did this come from?

Westwood The Australian police found it when, at our request, they searched Julie Tyson's apartment.

Vanessa (*intensely curious*) But what was in the other flight bag? The one that was destroyed?

Carl (*before Westwood can answer; almost a suggestion of derision in his voice*) You don't have to tell us! A soft toy—a Koala bear! Stuffed with drugs, no doubt!

Westwood (*smiling*) You're right about the Koala bear, Mr Houston. But this affair has got nothing to do with drugs. Nothing whatsoever. (*After a tiny pause*) Do you remember reading about an emerald necklace that was stolen? It was reputed to be the most valuable necklace in the world.

Carl Yes, of course. The papers were full of it. A fabulously wealthy South American—Baron something-or-other—bought it for his wife's collection.

Westwood That's right. The Concorde Necklace the media called it. The necklace was stolen whilst the baron and his entourage were being photographed, prior to boarding Concorde. How on earth it could have happened under those circumstances, I don't know. But it did! About a week ago I flew out to Rio to report to the baron. And a more Mafia-like character, I've never met! I told him that for some time now Scotland Yard have had their eyes on an international fence. I said we felt confident that the necklace would, ultimately, fall into this man's hands and that when that happened we'd be able to recover it. I didn't convince the baron, I'm afraid. *No way!* He made it quite clear he wasn't remotely interested in what *might* happen. We'd failed to find the necklace so, from now on, he was taking the law into his own hands. The day I returned to London I received a message from Sydney saying that an Australian named Harry Scottsdale had been in touch with the fence and appeared to be doing a deal with him. (*Looking at Carl*) The message also stated that an Englishman, Carl Houston, had recently become friendly with Scottsdale.

Carl Go on ...

Westwood Soon after your plane took off I spoke to the security people at Sydney airport. They reported that their examination of your flight bag had revealed a soft toy in the shape of a Koala bear. The bear was all dressed up and was wearing fake jewellery, including a necklace. The necklace was, in fact, the Concorde necklace which had been cleverly disguised so that it looked like the rest of the junk jewellery. For a time we were convinced that you were part of the set-up, Mr Houston. It was only this afternoon, after listening to a lengthy statement from Ronnie Sheldon, that I fully realized what had happened.

Vanessa Then the hijacking was just a coincidence, and had nothing to do with the necklace?

Westwood On the contrary, it had everything to do with the necklace. That's what the baron meant when he said he'd take the law into his own hands. His men suddenly discovered the necklace was on the plane and they boarded it at Melbourne. After refuelling at Singapore, they'd have instructed the pilot to fly to South America. Unfortunately, as so often happens in these cases, events got out of hand.

Vanessa But supposing the hijacking hadn't taken place? Supposing the original plan had been successful and the Koala bear hadn't been destroyed?

Westwood Then, once your husband had cleared customs, Ronnie Sheldon, who was working for Scottsdale, would have relieved him of the flight bag and delivered it to the fence. But the hijacking *did* happen—and not only that. (*To Carl*) You saved Sheldon's life which, believe me, had the most profound effect on him.

A brief, awkward silence

Carl Well—you've been very frank. I'll say that for you. Now, I'll be equally frank. What is it you want from me?

Westwood (*faintly amused*) What makes you think I want anything from you?

Carl Don't you?

Westwood (*after a moment*) With your permission, I'd like to have this room bugged.

Carl Bugged?

Westwood Yes, sir.
Carl Why?
Westwood Because now, more than ever, I'm interested in your friends, Mr Houston. And what they might say to you.
Carl OK! So it's bugged! (*With authority*) Then what? Then what happens?

Black-out

SCENE 3

The same. An hour later

Carl is sitting at his desk listening to a somewhat agitated Oliver who stands facing him. There is no sign of the flight bag

Oliver Believe me, Carl, I was staggered when that chap Westwood crawled out of the woodwork. At first, I couldn't make out who he was or what the devil he was talking about. Like you, I hadn't the slightest idea Harry was in London. (*A moment*) I suppose there's no doubt about all this? The man was Harry Scottsdale and not a look-alike?
Carl There's no doubt. It was Harry.

Pause

Oliver Westwood said he had a knife and you were struggling to get hold of it. Is that true?
Carl Yes, it is. I had to defend myself, I had no alternative.
Oliver And that's when he had the heart attack?
Carl Yes.

Pause

Oliver (*thoughtfully*) Well—that figures, I guess.
Carl What do you mean? That figures?
Oliver Harry had a heart attack about a year ago whilst on a visit to Canberra.

Carl rises and joins Oliver

Carl Are you sure?
Oliver I'm quite sure. He was told to take it easy for a while.
Carl Well, I'm relieved to hear that. It should make my story more credible.
Oliver (*after a brief pause*) Carl, what exactly did you tell that chap Westwood? About me, I mean?
Carl He asked me how I came to know Harry. I told him he was a friend of yours and that you'd given me a letter of introduction to him.
Oliver And that's all?
Carl Why, yes.
Oliver (*dismissing the matter*) Yes, well—that's rather what I thought. But he was so damned inquisitive. (*Shaking his head; a note of exasperation in his voice*) I've had a pretty awful day, one way and another. From the

moment I got up this morning everything seems to have gone wrong. My plane was two hours late leaving, then when we landed I had to cope with Westwood and finally—if that wasn't enough—I learnt that one of the girls in my office had committed suicide.

Carl Committed suicide?

Oliver Yes, and such a clever girl. I just can't imagine why she did it. I shall miss her terribly. She started with me way back, when I had a tiny office in Holborn. (*A sudden thought*) But wait a minute! You knew her! She stayed here over Christmas.

Carl (*taken-aback*) Margaret MacKenzie?

Oliver That's right.

Carl (*moving nearer Oliver; a note of disbelief in his voice*) She's committed suicide?

Oliver Yes. I'm afraid so.

Carl (*tensely*) When did this happen?

Oliver I think late this afternoon, but I'm not sure.

Carl How did she kill herself, do you know?

Oliver I understand she slashed her wrists, but—I don't know the full details. I only heard about it just over an hour ago when I phoned my secretary.

Carl (*after a sympathetic pause*) She was having an affair with Bernard. But I expect you knew that?

Oliver (*astonished*) Bernard?

Carl Yes.

Oliver No, I didn't know that. (*Slowly*) That does surprise me. Well, well! You can never tell what goes on these days.

A brief pause

Carl Come along, Oliver. I'll get one of the girls to show you to your room.

Oliver Thank you, Carl. And not to worry. We'll get to grips with this Scottsdale affair. I'll be more on the ball when I've had a shower. Supposing we meet again in an hour's time?

Carl Yes, that's fine. I'll be here. (*Indicating the patio*) Come across the garden. I'll have a nightcap waiting for you.

Ruth enters

Ruth Excuse me, Carl. (*To Oliver*) Do you think you could move your car for us, Mr Radford? It's in rather an awkward spot.

Oliver Yes, of course. Sorry about that.

Oliver exits with Carl

Ruth crosses to the desk, opens a drawer and takes out several files. She stands for a moment quietly studying them, finally returning two of the files to the drawer. Having done this she places the remaining files on top of the typewriter and picks it up

Bernard enters from the patio. He is still wearing outdoor clothes and appears distinctly satisfied with his visit to Bath and life in general

Ruth (*surprised to see him*) Hallo, Bernard!

Bernard Hi! What are you up to?

Ruth I'm moving back into my office. I've decided it's the only way I'll get rid of the decorators.

Bernard I told you that weeks ago.

Ruth Yes, I do believe you did, Bernard.

Ruth exits

Bernard looks around the room for a moment or two, smiling to himself. Then he crosses down to the hi-fi unit. He is staring at the instrument, his thoughts on the cassette

Carl returns

Carl If you're looking for the cassette, Bernard, it's here.

As Bernard quickly turns Carl takes the cassette out of his pocket and holds it up

What did you say you wanted for it?

Bernard I didn't say. But I think about thirty-five thousand would be a reasonable figure.

Carl You think thirty-five thousand would be a reasonable figure?

Bernard Yes, I do. (*He moves to the sofa*)

Carl Well, even if I were interested, how could I be sure that this is the only tape? You could have half a dozen of these things, for all I know.

Bernard (*very sure of himself; relaxing on the sofa*) That's the only one, and you'll have to take my word for it.

Carl I'm afraid your word doesn't carry much weight with me at the moment. (*Indicating the cassette*) However, this didn't impress me. It didn't impress me one little bit. And it won't impress the police either.

Bernard Don't be a damn fool! It proves you were lying. It proves, beyond a shadow of doubt, that you knew Harry Scottsdale was over here.

Carl It proves precisely nothing! It's not my voice on the tape, and you know it isn't. But we'll discuss that later. You and I have far more important things to talk about.

Bernard There's only one thing I want to talk about, and that's the thirty-five thousand!

Carl Bernard, you're very good at your job, and you're probably good at a lot of other things, but when it comes to blackmail you're an amateur. What do you think would happen if *I* went to the police and handed this thing over to them?

Bernard You?

Carl Yes. Supposing I took it to the inspector and told him that you'd tried to sell it to me. What do you think his reaction would be? I'll tell you! The first thing he would want to know——

Bernard (*rising, interrupting him*) Don't give me that bullshit. You're in trouble, Carl. After what's happened you daren't get within a hundred miles of the police.

Carl You think so! Well, you're wrong! You couldn't be more wrong! And I'll very quickly prove it to you. (*He crosses to the desk, picks up the phone and dials*)

Bernard stares at him, taken by surprise. A tense pause. Bernard is shaken. His self assurance gradually fades as he watches Carl. When Carl finishes dialling, Bernard rushes towards him in an attempt to knock the phone out of his hand. They are on the verge of a struggle

Ruth enters

Both men freeze

(*Sharply*) Yes? What is it, Ruth?

Ruth (*puzzled by their behaviour*) Excuse me, Carl. Mr Westwood is here.

Carl (*surprised*) Westwood? (*He looks at Bernard; slowly putting the phone down*) All right. I'll come along . . .

Ruth (*shaking her head*) He didn't ask for you. It's Bernard he wants to talk to.

Bernard (*taken aback*) Me? (*He stares at Carl, then at Ruth*) He wants to see me?

Ruth Yes, Bernard. I've just said so!

Carl (*after a moment*) Show him in, Ruth.

Ruth exits

Bernard This chap's from Scotland Yard. Why on earth does he want to see me?

Carl (*quietly*) You don't know why?

Bernard No. I don't.

Carl You've no idea?

Bernard No. Have you?

Pause

Carl I'm afraid you're in for a shock, Bernard.

Bernard (*alarmed*) Has something happened to Millie, or one of the boys?

Carl No.

Bernard Then what the devil is it? (*Pause*) Tell me!

There is an uneasy silence on Carl's part

Westwood enters

Westwood (*to Carl*) I'm sorry to disturb you, Mr Houston, but I'd like to have a word with Mr Decker.

Carl Yes, of course.

Carl moves towards the hall

Westwood No, please! Don't go. I'd rather you stay, sir. I was on my way back to London when I had a call from Chief Inspector Bradshaw. (*Turning towards Bernard*) I imagine you've heard from the inspector, sir?

Bernard No. Why should I hear from him?

Westwood (*ignoring the question*) No doubt he'll be in touch with you later.

Bernard Look—what is this? What's it all about?

Westwood It's about a friend of yours, sir. Margaret MacKenzie.

Bernard (*after an uneasy hesitation*) I know Miss MacKenzie, of course, but—you've got it wrong. She's a friend of my wife's.

Westwood Oh? Is that so, sir? I was under the impression she was a friend of yours. A very close friend.

Pause

Bernard Why are you interested in Miss MacKenzie?

Westwood (*his eyes on Bernard*) She's dead, sir.

Bernard is thunderstruck

Bernard (*hardly audible*) Dead?

Westwood It would appear she committed suicide.

Bernard When?

Westwood Late this afternoon.

Bernard I don't believe this! I just don't believe it!

Westwood It's true, I'm afraid.

Bernard But it can't be true! She'd never do a thing like that! Not Margaret!

Westwood Then what are you suggesting? That she was murdered?

Bernard I'm not suggesting anything. It's just that . . . Are you sure the girl you're talking about—the dead girl—is Margaret MacKenzie?

Westwood There's no doubt about it. She worked for Oliver Radford. (*Pause*) When did you last see Miss MacKenzie, sir?

Bernard hesitates, then decides to tell Westwood the truth

Bernard I saw her the day before yesterday. I had an appointment in London yesterday morning . . .

Westwood Go on, sir.

Bernard So I . . . stayed . . . the night at her flat . . .

Westwood Was that the first time you'd stayed there?

Bernard No.

Westwood You'd stayed there several times before?

Bernard nods

Have you a key to the apartment?

Bernard Er—yes, I have.

Westwood Perhaps you'd give it to me, sir?

Bernard looks at him, not sure how to treat this request. Finally he produces a key and hands it to Westwood

Thank you. (*Pause*) How was Miss MacKenzie when you last saw her? Was she worried or depressed in any way?

Bernard I—I don't think so.

Bernard, distinctly upset, sinks into one of the armchairs

Westwood Had she received any threatening letters, strange telephone calls, that sort of thing?

Bernard Not to my knowledge.

Westwood is studying Bernard

Westwood What have your movements been during the day? How did you spend this afternoon, sir?

Carl Bernard had the day off. He's thinking of opening a restaurant of his own in Bath and he drove over there.

Westwood Is that so? (*To Bernard*) When did you leave here?

Bernard This morning, about ten o'clock.

Westwood And what time did you get to Bath?

Bernard Oh—it must have been about a quarter to twelve.

Westwood Were you in Bath the whole day?

Bernard Yes. I didn't leave there until about seven o'clock.

Westwood Did you meet anyone whilst you were there?

Bernard Why, yes! I had several appointments. I was with people the whole time.

Westwood Right up to the time you left, which was approximately seven o'clock this evening?

Bernard (*worried; agitated*) Yes.

Westwood Thank you, sir. (*He turns to go*)

Carl You said just now, "it would appear" Miss MacKenzie committed suicide.

Westwood Her wrists were slashed, as a result of which she died. That's all I can tell you at the moment, I'm afraid.

Bernard (*horrified*) But Margaret would never do that! She'd be incapable of doing it! The sight of blood terrified her.

Westwood You'd be surprised what people can do to themselves, whilst under duress. (*Closing the interview*) But it's an interesting comment, nevertheless. (*Moving towards the hall*) Mr Decker ... Mr Houston ...

Carl joins Westwood and goes out into the hall with him

Bernard is now desperate and near to tears. Pause

Carl returns and stands for a second or two staring at Bernard. Finally, he crosses to the drinks cabinet, pours Bernard a large Scotch, and takes it down to him

Carl Drink this.

Bernard shakes his head

Drink it!

Bernard eventually looks up and takes the glass from him. Carl pulls one of the armchairs closer to Bernard and sits facing him. Pause

Tell me about Margaret MacKenzie.

Bernard drinks

Bernard (*evasively*) There's nothing to tell ...

Carl (*leaning towards him*) Tell me about her, Bernard!

Pause

Bernard We were having an affair.
Carl I know that. That's not what I'm asking you.

Pause

You told Westwood that you didn't think she'd committed suicide.
Bernard Yes, but ... (*He hesitates nervously*)
Carl But what? (*Pause*) Go on, Bernard.
Bernard I—I shouldn't have said that. It was stupid of me. I just wasn't thinking.
Carl But you're thinking now! Thinking fast! Aren't you, Bernard? (*A note of anger in his voice*) Margaret MacKenzie was murdered. You know that! We both know it! And what happened to Margaret can very easily happen to you!

A brief pause

Right now, my friend, you need help, and in spite of what's happened I'll do what I can for you. For Millie's sake, if for no other reason. But you've got to trust me. You've got to keep nothing back. (*Pause*) Now tell me the whole story.

Bernard's hands are shaking but he slowly finishes his drink and puts the glass down. He realizes that he has no alternative but to confide in Carl

Bernard I'd always wanted a restaurant of my own, but I could never raise the money. Then one night Margaret suggested that it might be possible for me to blackmail her boss, Oliver Radford. She told me that Radford had deliberately created the tycoon image in order to conceal his real activities which was the handling of stolen property.
Carl And whose idea was it to blackmail me as well as Oliver?
Bernard It was Margaret's! I swear to you it was Margaret's idea. She even produced the tape.
Carl Miss MacKenzie seems to have thought of everything. Except the one thing that really mattered. Her own safety. (*Pause*) What was Oliver's reaction when you confronted him?
Bernard He was surprised, but he kept his cool and offered to think over what I'd said. Later that day he telephoned and said there was no problem and he'd be in touch. He spoke to me again the next morning. He said he was leaving for Amsterdam but I would be receiving a banker's draft and I should go ahead with the property.
Carl Did you receive the banker's draft?
Bernard No, but I spoke to him early this morning. He told me not to worry, there'd been a slight hiccup, but he promised I'd receive the money within the next four or five days.
Carl And you believed him?
Bernard Yes, I believed him. (*Pause*) But—that was before I knew about Margaret.

Carl (*shaking his head*) You won't get the money. He's not the slightest intention of giving it to you. He's just waiting for you to get to the point of no return over the property deal. To what extent are you committed?

Bernard To be honest, I'm not sure. There are still some papers I haven't signed.

Carl Well, I said I'd help you, and I will. You can keep your job for as long as it takes to sort out the mess you're in. But first, there's something you must do for me. (*Tiny pause*) Oliver Radford's here, he's staying the night.

Bernard (*surprised*) I didn't realize that!

Carl He came straight from the airport where he was questioned about Harry Scottsdale. He's rattled. Quite badly rattled. We've had one meeting and we're due to have another. However, before that happens I want you to talk to him. I want you to tell him that my flight bag wasn't destroyed. I want you to tell him that it's here, in the apartment . . .

Bernard Here?

Carl Yes. Tell him you've seen the bag. And the Koala bear . . .

The Lights quickly fade to Black-out

SCENE 4

The same. Later that evening

The curtains are drawn back and the window leading on to the patio is open

Carl is at the desk attempting to write a letter. He eventually abandons the task, rises, and crosses to the window. His manner is nervous, a shade tense, as he stands looking out at the patio. Pause. There is a buzz on the intercom phone and Carl quickly returns to the desk. It is the call he has been waiting for

Carl (*on the phone*) Bernard? . . . (*Tensely*) What happened? (*A long pause*) I see . . . (*He replaces the phone and turns away from the desk*)

Ruth enters from the hall. She is carrying a copy of a new wine list

Ruth Can you spare a minute?

Carl Well—only a minute, Ruth.

Ruth I've written to the Customs and Excise people, as you suggested, but I can't find the VAT form. I think you must have it, Carl.

Carl (*shaking his head*) I haven't got it.

Ruth You haven't?

Carl No.

Ruth Then I'll take another look. But if you do come across it let me have it. And don't forget to sign it. We could be in trouble. We should have sent it off days ago.

Carl (*dismissing her*) Yes, all right, Ruth.

Ruth (*putting the wine list down on a chair*) Here's the new wine list. Vanessa's checking the prices.

Carl Yes, Ruth . . . (*He turns away from her*)

A moment, then realizing that Carl doesn't wish to talk, Ruth moves towards the hall. She suddenly remembers something

Ruth Oh, by the way. I saw a friend of yours this afternoon.

Carl turns

Mr Sheldon.

Carl (*surprised*) Ronnie Sheldon? Where did you see him?

Ruth In the village. I was visiting a friend of mine.

Carl Are you sure it was Ronnie Sheldon?

Ruth Quite sure. We waved to each other.

Ruth exits

There is an appreciable pause, during which it is obvious that Carl is thinking of what Ruth has just told him. Eventually he picks up the wine list and returns to the desk. Somewhat absent-mindedly Carl starts tidying the desk, obviously giving himself something to do before the arrival of Oliver. He gathers up various documents and is about to place them in a drawer when he suddenly comes across the VAT form

Carl stares at the form for a moment, then with an irritated shake of the head, he signs it and goes out into the hall with it

Long pause

Oliver enters from the patio. He has showered and changed and looks very sure of himself, as if ready to deal with any problem which may arise. He takes stock of the room, somewhat surprised to find it deserted, finally moving towards the bedroom

Oliver (*calling*) Carl!

Receiving no reply he crosses the room again and looks out into the hall. Pause. As Oliver turns his back on the hall and moves slowly down to the sofa, he takes a gun out of his pocket and briefly examines it. He replaces the gun and is about to sit on the sofa

Carl enters

Carl Sorry, Oliver.

Oliver turns

Oliver That's all right, dear boy.

Carl I've been having a word with Ruth. (*Indicating the drinks cabinet*) Now—what sort of a nightcap would you like?

Oliver Thank you. I don't think I'll have anything at the moment.

Carl You're sure?

Oliver Quite sure.

Pause

Carl Shortly after you left the police questioned Bernard about Margaret MacKenzie.

Oliver Is that so? Well—if he was having an affair with her that was to be expected, I suppose. I imagine it won't be long before they start on me since the poor girl worked for my outfit. Not that I can help them, I was in Amsterdam when it happened.

Carl I got the impression that the police are not too happy about the affair. I have a feeling there's a doubt in their minds as to whether it was suicide.

Oliver Really? That does surprise me. What else could it have been?

Carl Well—murder, I suppose. It's the only other possibility.

Oliver Murder? (*Thoughtfully*) That never occurred to me. (*Pause*) I've had another word with my secretary, by the way. Apparently there was no sign of a struggle, Margaret's body was found in the bathroom and the door was locked from the inside. That doesn't sound very much like murder, does it?

Carl No, it doesn't.

Slight pause

Oliver Did you and Vanessa see much of Margaret when she stayed here?

Carl Very little. She was out most days. She did join us for a drink one evening but there were several other people present and I didn't really get a chance to talk to her. She struck Vanessa as being a very capable person.

Oliver She was. Extremely capable. We shall miss her.

Carl I'm sure. (*Brief pause*) Was she well off, do you know?

Oliver It depends what you mean by that. She was certainly well paid. Why do you ask?

Carl It's just that, I was thinking—if she was murdered, then obviously there must have been a motive.

Oliver Yes, of course. But the same thing applies if she wasn't murdered. She must have had a reason, a motive if you like, for taking her own life. (*A pause*) I must admit, I was very surprised to learn that she'd been friendly with Bernard. How long had that been going on, do you know?

Carl I gather from Vanessa this was the second time round, they'd had an affair some time back.

Oliver (*pause*) Talking about a motive, Carl. Whilst I was under the shower I started thinking about Harry Scottsdale and what possible reason he could have had for wanting to kill you. What was *his* motive, I wonder? Have you any idea?

Carl Yes, I have. At least—(*after a moment's consideration*)—I have a theory. It's only a theory, but it seems to make sense. To me, at any rate.

Oliver What is your theory?

Carl I doubt whether it will impress you.

Oliver (*quietly*) Try me.

A significant pause

Carl It's my belief Harry Scottsdale was doing a deal over a valuable emerald necklace. The Concorde Necklace, in fact. The police were on the look out for the necklace because, apart from anything else, they felt sure it would lead them to a highly successful fence. A man they'd been trying to get their hands on for some considerable time.

Oliver Go on, Carl . . .

Carl The necklace was sent to the fence by means of a soft toy, a Koala bear, which—unbeknown to me—was in the flight bag I was carrying. Quite out of the blue, and by sheer coincidence, I mentioned a Koala bear to Ronnie Sheldon and he became suspicious. Almost immediately after my remark the hijacking took place and the flight bag and its contents were destroyed.

Pause

Oliver (*quietly*) Go on.

Carl It's my opinion Harry Scottsdale didn't believe Sheldon's account of what happened on the plane. He was convinced I knew about the Koala bear and that I'd rescued my flight bag. That's why he came here. To get the necklace and stop me from talking.

Pause

Oliver And that's it? That's your theory?

Carl Yes.

Oliver Well, it's an interesting theory, I'll say that.

Carl I'm glad you think so. Now, let's have your opinion, Oliver. What do *you* think?

Oliver What do *I* think?

Carl Yes. Am I right? (*Brief pause*) Am I right about Harry?

There is a deliberate silence on Oliver's part

Oliver Yes, you're right. He was convinced you had the necklace. Totally convinced. But, like a fool, I didn't go along with him.

The two men are eyeing each other

Carl, I don't know what you're up to. I don't know what the devil you're playing at. But whatever it is, take my advice, and forget it. Forget it, and hand over the necklace. Now! Before it's too late.

Carl Too late, for what?

Oliver I think you know what happened to Margaret MacKenzie—on my instructions. I'd rather it didn't happen to you, Carl. But it will, make no mistake about that! Unless I get the necklace!

Carl I'm afraid I can't give you the necklace.

Oliver (*the first sign of intense anger*) You can't? Why not?

Carl Because I haven't got it. Both the flight bag and the Koala bear were destroyed when the plane caught fire.

Oliver That's not true!

Carl It is true, Oliver.

Oliver It's not true! You're lying!

Carl (*with quiet sincerity*) I haven't got the flight bag, the Koala bear, or the necklace.

Oliver (*furious*) You're lying! I know you're lying! Bernard's seen the flight bag! (*Taking the gun from his pocket*) Now fetch it, Carl!

Carl freezes. A tense pause

Fetch me the flight bag!

Carl hesitates

If you don't do what I say, I shall use this! I shan't hesitate! Not for one God-damn minute! Now get me the flight bag!

Carl is badly shaken, not only by the gun, but by the extent of Oliver's wrath and hostility. He is thinking fast, trying to decide how to deal with the situation

Vanessa appears from the patio. She stares at the gun in astonishment

Vanessa Oliver!

Carl makes a quick movement towards Vanessa but Oliver stops him with the gun

Oliver (*frenzied*) Stay where you are! (*He rushes towards Vanessa and, grabbing hold of her, holds the gun dangerously near her head*)

Tense pause

Now you heard what I said! Get me the flight bag!

Carl stares at him, then at a terrified Vanessa. He is desperate, undecided what to do

Carl All right, I'll get it. But first, move away from Vanessa!
Oliver (*heated; shaking his head*) No! First—you do what I've told you!
Carl For God's sake! (*With authority*) Now, release her and I'll fetch the bag!

A tense pause, then Oliver moves away from Vanessa. She makes an instinctive movement in the direction of Carl but Oliver immediately threatens her with the gun. Vanessa freezes, midway between the two men

Oliver Go and stand by the desk.

Pause

Carl (*watching Oliver*) Do as he says, Vanessa.

Vanessa crosses to the desk

Oliver (*to Carl*) Now get the bag!

Carl looks at Vanessa, attempting to reassure her, then he turns and goes quickly into the bedroom

Oliver moves a shade nearer Vanessa. She backs away from him. Long, tense silence. The phone rings. Pause. Vanessa stares at the phone, it is almost as if she is trying to make up her mind whether to answer it or not

Let it ring!

The phone continues ringing. Finally it stops. Oliver takes his eyes off Vanessa and looks towards the bedroom

Carl enters, carrying the flight bag

(*Indicating one of the armchairs*) Put the bag on that chair.

Carl, both hesitant and nervous, does so. Oliver crosses to the chair with the gun levelled at Carl

Oliver Open it!

Carl pauses, then zips open the flight bag and moves quickly away from the chair. Oliver peers inside the bag, then starts searching it. There is a stunned silence, before a furious-looking Oliver turns on Carl

Where's the necklace?
Carl I told you. I haven't got it.
Oliver You're lying! (*He is beside himself with anger. He raises the gun*)
Carl Wait! Oliver, wait!

Oliver hesitates. A tense silence

All right. (*A shrug of defeat*) I'll get you the necklace. But it'll take some time.
Oliver Why?
Carl It's in a safe in the bedroom. The safe's hidden.
Oliver (*glancing at Vanessa*) Is he telling the truth?
Vanessa Yes! Yes, he is! It's behind the bed.

Oliver stares at Carl for a second or two

Oliver OK! Go ahead!
Carl I shall need the key.

Before Oliver can protest, Carl moves to the desk and starts to open a drawer. Watched by a slightly suspicious Oliver, he searches several drawers before finally producing a key. He holds the key up, for Oliver to see, then crosses towards the bedroom

Oliver (*stopping him*) Let me see that!

A moment, then Carl hands him the key. Pause

This doesn't look like a safe key.
Carl I know. But it is. It's a wall safe.

A moment—then with a satisfied nod Oliver returns the key. Carl takes the key from him, then "accidentally" drops it. He bends down to pick it up and as he does so he suddenly throws himself against Oliver's legs, at the same time knocking the gun out of his hand. There is a tense moment as both men endeavour to get their hands on the weapon. The struggle is brought to an end by a blow from Oliver, deliberately aimed at Carl's shoulder

Carl, in obvious pain, backs away. He is holding his shoulder as Oliver recovers the gun and faces him with it. It is obvious from the expression on Oliver's face that he intends to use it. Vanessa screams. A shot is heard. Carl reacts to the sound of the shot as Vanessa rushes across to him. Then, utterly astonished, they both stare at Oliver. Their astonishment turns to incredulity

*as Oliver, clutching his chest, staggers forward, finally collapsing. There is a
pause, then Carl and Vanessa look towards the patio*

   Ronnie Sheldon appears. He is holding a gun. He moves slowly down to Carl

Ronnie What do you say to a man who, at great risk to himself, drags you
   off a burning aircraft . . . ?
Carl Thanks very much, old chap. I'll do the same for you next time . . .

Carl takes the gun out of Ronnie's hand as the Lights fade to Blackout

                                     Curtain

FURNITURE AND PROPERTY LIST

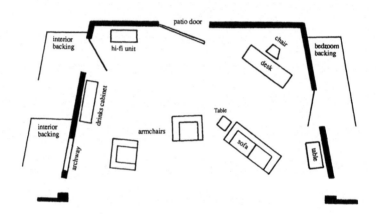

garden backing

patio door

interior backing

hi-fi unit

chair

bedroom backing

interior backing

drinks cabinet

archway

armchairs

Table

desk

sofa

table

ACT I

SCENE 1

On stage: 2 aircraft seats
Book (for **Carl**)

Personal: **Ronnie:** wrist-watch (worn throughout)
Carl: wrist-watch (worn throughout)
Man: automatic rifle

SCENE 2

On stage: Armchairs
Sofa
Tables. *On one:* cigarette box with cigarettes, ashtray
Hi-fi unit
Drinks cabinet. *In it:* bottle of Scotch, glasses, ashtray
Desk. *On it:* intercom system, telephones, business accessories, pens, notepad, typewriter, stiletto-type letter opener. *In drawer:* key, folder containing papers
Chair
Curtains open at window

Personal: **Westwood:** CID identity photo-card, wrist-watch (worn throughout)

SCENE 3

On stage: As SCENE 2

Off stage: Menu **(Bernard)**
Account book **(Ruth)**

Personal: **Ruth:** wrist-watch (worn throughout)
Millie: handbag

SCENE 4

Set: Papers, letters, accounts, etc. on desk
Pile of correspondence for **Ruth**

SCENE 5

On stage: As SCENE 4

Off stage: Briefcase containing bulky documents **(Oliver)**
Tray with pot of coffee, cream, sugar, 2 cups, saucers and spoons **(Bernard)**

SCENE 6

Strike: Tray and contents

Re-set: Curtains closed at window

Off stage: Tray with tea things **(Vanessa)**
Towel, first-aid box **(Vanessa)**

Personal: **Carl:** half-smoked cigarette
Man: switchblade knife in pocket, blood sac, mask

ACT II

SCENE 1

Strike: Tray with tea things
Towel
First-aid box
Switchblade knife

Re-set: Curtains open at window
Files containing papers on desk

Off stage: Letters **(Ruth)**

Personal: **Bernard:** cassette tape in pocket, wrist-watch

SCENE 2

Re-set: Curtains closed at window

Offstage: Dress in plastic cover **(Millie)**
Large packaged box containing a flight bag with various contents **(Ruth)**

Scene 3

Strike: Wrapping paper, box, flight bag and contents

Re-set: Window curtains closed

Personal: **Carl:** cassette tape in pocket
              Bernard: key in pocket

Scene 4

Re-set: Window curtains and window open

Off stage: Wine list **(Ruth)**
           Flight bag **(Carl)**

Personal: **Oliver:** gun
          Ronnie: gun

LIGHTING PLOT

Practical fittings required: desk and table lamps

Interior

ACT I, SCENE 1. Night

To open: Black-out

Cue 1   When ready   (Page 1)
         Bring up subdued lighting on two aircraft seats

Cue 2   The figure of a man emerges from the darkness   (Page 3)
         Quick fade to black-out

ACT I, SCENE 2. Evening

To open: Practicals on, evening light from window

Cue 3   **Westwood:** "I think he's lying. . . ."   (Page 8)
         Black-out

ACT I, SCENE 3. Morning

To open: General daylight

Cue 4   **Vanessa** stares after **Carl**   (Page 17)
         Fade to black-out

ACT I, SCENE 4. Night

To open: Practicals on, night effect through window

Cue 5   **Ronnie** exits   (Page 21)
         Fade quickly to black-out

ACT I, SCENE 5. Morning

To open: General daylight

Cue 6   **Bernard:** "I know about the Koala bear."   (Page 27)
         Black-out

ACT I, SCENE 6. Night

To open: One table lamp with covering spot; light spill from kitchen and
           bedroom

No cues

ACT II, SCENE 1.   Morning

To open: General daylight

Cue 7   **Vanessa:** "And you lied to me!"   (Page 41)
           Quick fade to black-out

ACT II, SCENE 2.   Evening

To open: All practicals on with covering spots; light spill from hall,
           evening effect outside window

Cue 8   **Carl:** "Then what happens?"   (Page 50)
           Black-out

ACT II, SCENE 3.   Evening

To open: All practicals on with covering spots; light spill from hall,
           evening effect outside window

Cue 9   **Carl:** "And the Koala bear ..."   (Page 57)
           Quick fade to black-out

ACT II, SCENE 4.   Evening

To open: All practicals on with covering spots; light spill from hall,
           evening effect outside window

Cue 10   **Carl** takes the gun out of **Ronnie**'s hand   (Page 63)
           Fade to black-out

EFFECTS PLOT

Note: the cues for the sound of the front door opening and closing are not given in this plot. It is suggested that a door slam be used by individual actors as they enter or exit via the hallway

ACT I

ACT II

MADE AND PRINTED IN GREAT BRITAIN BY
LATIMER TREND & COMPANY LTD PLYMOUTH
MADE IN ENGLAND